PANTRY STUFFERS™

Rehydration Calculations Made Easy

U.S. MEASUREMENTS

Wanda Bailey Clark

6300 Creedmoor Road
Suite 170, Box 238
Raleigh, NC 27612

Limit of Liability/Disclaimer of Warranty
To the best of our knowledge, the calculations in this book are accurate for ordinary use and users. While Pantry Stuffers, LLC has used its best efforts in preparing this book, it makes no presentations or warranties of merchantability or fitness for a particular purpose. No warranty may be created or extended by sales representatives or written sales materials. The advice and strategies contained herein may not be suitable for your situation. You should consult with a professional where appropriate. Neither the publisher nor Pantry Stuffers, LLC shall be liable for any loss of profit or any other commercial damages, including but not limited to special, incidental, or other damages.

Disclaimer
The measurements within the tables are to be used as a practical guide in calculating how to replace fresh, canned, or frozen products with dehydrated, freeze-dried, dried, or powdered products in your recipes. In some cases, measurements have been rounded up or down slightly to align to standard measurement instruments. Because dehydrated, freeze-dried, and powdered products are organic—the exact amount of water needed for reconstitution may vary slightly based on the amount of water present in the original product prior to processing.

Edited by Edie Mourey www.furrowpress.com

Cover and interior design by David G. Danglis / Pinwheel Creative

Front cover photo: www.istockphoto.com / karimala.
Interior photo: www.istockphoto.com / marilyna.

Printed in the United States of America
Library of Congress Control Number: 2013943204
International Standard Book Number: 978-0-9837561-6-3

Dedication

Every part of this cookbook is dedicated first to Jesus Christ, my Lord and Savior. I pray that this honors Him.

I give honor and appreciation to my husband, Paul, and to my family (David, Bobbie, and Trey) who are my greatest cheerleaders for EVERY project I undertake.

To my beloved friend and business partner, Steve Moore, thank you for handling all of the details behind the scenes and sharing the responsibility for bringing the vision God gave us to reality. To Jen, my friend and Steve's beautiful wife, thank you for all you do to help and encourage both of us through every step of this journey. We wouldn't be here without you!

Table of Recipes

Table of Recipes, cont'd.

Reconstitution

I am a busy suburban wife, mother, and grandmother with a passion for preparedness. While I have always been aware that dehydrated, freeze-dried, and powdered ingredients existed, I only started using them several years ago.

Not only do I package mixes for convenience and disaster support, but I also keep my pantry stuffed with a variety of products that I use to avoid a last-minute trip to the grocery store. Additionally, I maintain a supply to have a nutritious alternative for out-of-season vegetables.

The amount of water needed to reconstitute products is based on how much water was removed during the dehydration, freeze-drying, or powder process. Reconstitution is different product to product.

The purpose of this book is to meet a need I continually experience—especially for last-minute substitutions—how much product and how much water to add!

I hope that this book becomes a valuable tool to you, too, as you incorporate dried products into your pantry!

— Wanda Bailey Clark

The Basics

This book contains rehydration tables for "typical" reconstitution for the products listed. Please note that the reconstitution formula used to calculate the amounts of water and product to add is listed at the bottom of each table. If your product shows a different reconstitution formula, you will need to adjust your calculations.

Dehydration

Dehydration is the oldest, most natural form of food preservation. Ancient civilizations used various forms of open-air drying to dry vegetables and fruits to preserve food for future use. Modern dehydrators use controlled air and heat to effectively remove the moisture content from vegetables and fruits.

Freeze-Drying Process

Freeze-drying is dehydration that works by freezing and then reducing the pressure to allow the frozen water in the material to sublimate directly from the solid phase to the gas phase.

Powder Process

The more you dry a product, the more stable and less susceptible it is to nutritional loss. There are many different processes used to create powdered products. Advances in freeze-drying and spray technologies are constantly adding to the number and variety of powdered food products available. Like the dehydration and freeze-drying processes, food products are powdered when their nutritional value is at its peak.

In addition to fruit and vegetable powders, powdered processes include dairy, syrups, honey, seasonings, and wine.

Nutritional Value

Most vitamins and minerals remain intact during the dehydration process, except for vitamin C which does not tolerate the dehydration process. Dehydration retains more vitamin and mineral content than canned or frozen vegetables. It has also been suggested by many that, in some cases, if the fresh produce in the grocery store has been picked while green and has traveled for days before arriving at the store, then dehydrated vegetables even have a higher vitamin and mineral content than their fresh counterparts.

Measurement Tables

U.S. Measurements

	Teaspoon	Tablespoon	Cup
1 Teaspoon	1	1/3	1/48
1 Tablespoon	3	1	1/16
1/8 cup	6	2	1/8
1/6 cup	8	2 2/3	1/6
1/4 cup	12	4	1/4
1/3 cup	16	5 1/3	1/3
3/8 cup	18	6	3/8
1/2 cup	24	8	1/2
2/3 cup	32	10 2/3	2/3
3/4 cup	36	12	3/4
1 cup	48	16	1

Metric Measurements

US	Metric	Imperial
1/4 teaspoon	1 ml	
1/2 teaspoon	2.5 ml	
1 teaspoon	5 ml	
1 1/2 teaspoon	7.5 ml	
1 Tablespoon	15 ml	
1/8 cup	30 ml	1 fl oz
1/4 cup	59 ml	2 fl oz
1/3 cup	79 ml	2.5 fl oz
1/2 cup	118.5 ml	4 fl oz
2/3 cup	158 ml	5 fl oz
3/4 cup	178 ml	6 fl oz
1 cup	237 ml	8 fl oz
2 cups (1 pint)	474 ml	16 fl oz
1 quart	1 liter	32 fl oz

NOTE: The U.S. conversion charts within this book are rounded to the nearest 1/4 tsp.

Vegetables

Asparagus, Freeze-Dried

Amount	Product	Water
1 cup	1 cup	2 cups
3/4 cup	3/4 cup	1 1/2 cups
1/2 cup	1/2 cup	1 cup
1/3 cup	1/3 cup	2/3 cup
1/4 cup	1/4 cup	1/2 cup
1 TBS	1 TBS	2 TBS
1 1/2 tsp	1 1/2 tsp	1 TBS
1 tsp	1 tsp	2 tsp

1 cup asparagus + 2 cups water = 1 cup asparagus

Bell Peppers, Dehydrated

Amount	Product	Water
1 cup	3/8 cup + 1 tsp	3/4 cup + 2 1/2 tsp
3/4 cup	1/4 cup + 2 1/2 tsp	1/2 cup + 5 tsp
1/2 cup	1/8 cup + 4 tsp	3/8 cup + 1 tsp
1/3 cup	1/8 cup + 1/2 tsp	1/4 cup + 1 tsp
1/4 cup	1 TBS + 1 tsp	1/8 cup + 4 tsp
1 TBS	1 1/4 tsp	2 1/2 tsp
1 1/2 tsp	1 tsp	1 1/4 tsp
1 tsp	1/2 tsp	1 tsp

1 cup peppers + 2 cups water = 2 1/2 cups peppers

Bell Peppers, Freeze-Dried

Amount	Product	Water
1 cup	1 cup	2 cups
3/4 cup	3/4 cup	1 1/2 cups
1/2 cup	1/2 cup	1 cup
1/3 cup	1/3 cup	2/3 cup
1/4 cup	1/4 cup	1/2 cup
1 TBS	1 TBS	2 TBS
1 1/2 tsp	1 1/2 tsp	1 TBS
1 tsp	1 tsp	2 tsp

1 cup peppers + 2 cups water = 1 cup peppers

Broccoli, Dehydrated

Amount	Product	Water
1 cup	1/4 cup + 1 TBS	1/2 cup + 1/8 cup
3/4 cup	1/8 cup + 5 tsp	3/8 cup + 4 tsp
1/2 cup	1/8 cup + 1 1/2 tsp	1/4 cup + 1 TBS
1/3 cup	1 TBS + 2 tsp	1/8 cup + 4 tsp
1/4 cup	1 TBS + 1 tsp	1/8 cup + 1 1/2 tsp
1 TBS	1 tsp	2 tsp
1 1/2 tsp	1/2 tsp	1 tsp
1 tsp	1/4 tsp	1/2 tsp

1 cup broccoli + 2 cups water = 3 1/4 cups broccoli

Broccoli, Freeze-Dried

Amount	Product	Water
1 cup	1/2 cup	1 1/2 cups
3/4 cup	3/8 cup	1 1/8 cups
1/2 cup	1/4 cup	3/4 cup
1/3 cup	1/8 cup + 2 tsp	1/2 cup
1/4 cup	1/8 cup	3/8 cup
1 TBS	1 1/2 tsp	1 TBS + 1 1/2 tsp
1 1/2 tsp	1 tsp	2 1/2 tsp
1 tsp	1/2 tsp	2 tsp

1/4 cup broccoli + 3/4 cup water = 1/2 cup broccoli

Cabbage, Dehydrated

Amount	Product	Water
1 cup	1/4 cup + 2 tsp	1/2 cup + 3 1/2 tsp
3/4 cup	1/8 cup + 4 1/2 tsp	3/8 cup + 1 TBS
1/2 cup	1/8 cup + 1 tsp	1/4 cup + 2 tsp
1/3 cup	1 TBS + 2 tsp	1/8 cup + 1 TBS
1/4 cup	1 TBS + 1/2 tsp	1/8 cup + 1 tsp
1 TBS	1 tsp	2 tsp
11/2 tsp	1/2 tsp	1 tsp
1 tsp	1/4 tsp	1/2 tsp

1 cup cabbage + 2 cups water = 3 1/2 cups cabbage

Cabbage, Freeze-Dried

Amount	Product	Water
1 cup	1/2 cup	1 1/2 cups
3/4 cup	3/8 cup	1 1/8 cups
1/2 cup	1/4 cup	3/4 cup
1/3 cup	1/8 cup + 2 tsp	1/2 cup
1/4 cup	1/8 cup	3/8 cup
1 TBS	1 1/2 tsp	1 TBS + 1 1/3 tsp
1 1/2 tsp	1 tsp	2 1/2 tsp
1 tsp	1/2 tsp	2 tsp

1/4 cup cabbage + 3/4 cup water = 1/2 cup cabbage

Carrots, Dehydrated

Amount	Product	Water
1 cup	1/4 cup	1/2 cup
3/4 cup	1/8 cup + 1 TBS	3/8 cup
1/2 cup	1/8 cup	1/4 cup
1/3 cup	1 TBS + 1 tsp	1/8 cup + 2 tsp
1/4 cup	1 TBS	1/8 cup
1 TBS	1 tsp	1 1/2 tsp
1 1/2 tsp	1/2 tsp	1 tsp
1 tsp	1/4 tsp	1/2 tsp

1 cup carrots + 2 cups water = 4 cups carrots

Carrots, Freeze-Dried

Amount	Product	Water
1 cup	3/8 cup	1 cup
3/4 cup	1/4 cup + 1 1/2 tsp	3/4 cup
1/2 cup	3 TBS	1/2 cup
1/3 cup	2 TBS	1/3 cup
1/4 cup	1 TBS + 1 1/2 tsp	1/4 cup
1 TBS	1 tsp	1 TBS
1 1/2 tsp	1/2 tsp	1 1/2 tsp
1 tsp	1/3 tsp	1 tsp

3 TBS carrots + 1/2 cups water = 1/2 cup carrots

Cauliflower, Dehydrated

Amount	Product	Water
1 cup	1/4 cup + 1 TBS	1/2 cup + 1/8 cup
3/4 cup	1/8 cup + 5 tsp	3/8 cup + 4 tsp
1/2 cup	1/8 cup + 1 1/2 tsp	1/4 cup + 3 tsp
1/3 cup	1 TBS + 2 tsp	1/8 cup + 4 tsp
1/4 cup	1 TBS + 1 tsp	1/8 cup + 1 1/2 tsp
1 TBS	1 tsp	2 tsp
1 1/2 tsp	1/2 tsp	1 tsp
1 tsp	1/4 tsp	1/2 tsp

1 cup cauliflower + 2 cups water = 3 1/4 cups cauliflower

Cauliflower, Freeze-Dried

Amount	Product	Water
1 cup	1/2 cup	1 1/2 cups
3/4 cup	3/8 cup	1 1/8 cups
1/2 cup	1/4 cup	3/4 cup
1/3 cup	1/8 cup + 2 tsp	1/2 cup
1/4 cup	1/8 cup	3/8 cup
1 TBS	1 1/2 tsp	1 TBS + 1 1/2 tsp
1 1/2 tsp	1 tsp	2 1/2 tsp
1 tsp	1/2 tsp	2 tsp

1/4 cup cauliflower + 3/4 cup water = 1/2 cup cauliflower

Celery, Dehydrated

Amount	Product	Water
1 cup	1/4 cup + 1 TBS	1/2 cup + 1/8 cup
3/4 cup	1/8 cup + 5 tsp	3/8 cup + 4 tsp
1/2 cup	1/8 cup + 1 1/2 tsp	1/4 cup + 3 tsp
1/3 cup	1 TBS + 2 tsp	1/8 cup + 4 tsp
1/4 cup	1 TBS + 1 tsp	1/8 cup + 1 1/2 tsp
1 TBS	1 tsp	2 tsp
1 1/2 tsp	1/2 tsp	1 tsp
1 tsp	1/4 tsp	1/2 tsp

1 cup celery + 2 cups water = 3 1/4 cups celery

Celery, Freeze-Dried

Amount	Product	Water
1 cup	1 cup	3 cups
3/4 cup	3/4 cup	2 1/4 cups
1/2 cup	1/2 cup	1 1/2 cups
1/3 cup	1/3 cup	1 cup
1/4 cup	1/4 cup	3/4 cup
1 TBS	1 TBS	1/8 cup + 1 TBS
1 1/2 tsp	1 1/2 tsp	1 TBS + 1 1/2 tsp
1 tsp	1 tsp	1 TBS

1/3 cup celery + 1 cup water = 1/3 cup celery (drain excess water)

Chives, Dehydrated

Amount	Product	Water
1 cup	1 cup	2 cups
3/4 cup	3/4 cup	1 1/2 cups
1/2 cup	1/2 cup	1 cup
1/3 cup	1/3 cup	2/3 cup
1/4 cup	1/4 cup	1/2 cup
1 TBS	1 TBS	1/8 cup
1 1/2 tsp	1 1/2 tsp	1 TBS
1 tsp	1 tsp	2 tsp

1 cup chives + 2 cups water = 1 cup chives

Chives, Freeze-Dried

Amount	Product	Water
1 cup	1 cup	2 cups
3/4 cup	3/4 cup	1 1/2 cups
1/2 cup	1/2 cup	1 cup
1/3 cup	1/3 cup	2/3 cup
1/4 cup	1/4 cup	1/2 cup
1 TBS	1 TBS	1/8 cup
1 1/2 tsp	1 1/2 tsp	1 TBS
1 tsp	1 tsp	2 tsp

1 cup chives + 2 cups water = 1 cup chives

Corn, Dehydrated

Amount	Product	Water
1 cup	1/2 cup	1 cup
3/4 cup	3/8 cup	3/4 cup
1/2 cup	1/4 cup	1/2 cup
1/3 cup	1/8 cup + 2 tsp	1/3 cup
1/4 cup	1/8 cup	1/4 cup
1 TBS	1 1/2 tsp	1 TBS
1 1/2 tsp	1 tsp	1 1/2 tsp
1 tsp	1/2 tsp	1 tsp

1 cup corn + 2 cups water = 2 cups corn

Corn, Freeze-Dried

Amount	Product	Water
1 cup	1 cup	2 cups
3/4 cup	3/4 cup	1 1/2 cups
1/2 cup	1/2 cup	1 cup
1/3 cup	1/3 cup	2/3 cup
1/4 cup	1/4 cup	1/2 cup
1 TBS	1 TBS	1/8 cup
1 1/2 tsp	1 1/2 tsp	1 TBS
1 tsp	1 tsp	2 tsp

1 cup corn + 2 cups water = 1 cup corn

Garlic, Dehydrated

Amount	Product	Water
1 cup	1/3 cup	2/3 cup
3/4 cup	1/4 cup	1/2 cup
1/2 cup	1/8 cup + 2 tsp	1/3 cup
1/3 cup	1 TBS + 2 1/2 tsp	3 TBS + 2 tsp
1/4 cup	1 TBS + 1 tsp	1/8 cup + 2 tsp
1 TBS	1 tsp	2 tsp
1 1/2 tsp	1/2 tsp	1 tsp
1 tsp	1/4 tsp	3/4 tsp

1 cup garlic + 2 cups water = 3 cups garlic

Garlic Recipe Substitutions for 1 clove of Garlic

- 1 tsp chopped garlic
- 1/2 tsp minced garlic
- 1/8 tsp garlic powder
- 1/2 tsp garlic flakes
- 1/4 tsp granulated garlic
- 1/2 tsp garlic juice

Green Beans, Dehydrated

Amount	Product	Water
1 cup	1/3 cup	2/3 cup
3/4 cup	1/4 cup	1/2 cup
1/2 cup	1/8 cup + 2 tsp	1/3 cup
1/3 cup	1 TBS + 2 1/2 tsp	3 TBS + 2 tsp
1/4 cup	1 TBS + 1 tsp	1/8 cup + 2 tsp
1 TBS	1 tsp	2 tsp
1 1/2 tsp	1/2 tsp	1 tsp
1 tsp	1/4 tsp	3/4 tsp

1 cup green beans + 2 cups water = 3 cups green beans

Green Beans, Freeze-Dried

Amount	Product	Water
1 cup	1/3 cup	1 cup
3/4 cup	1/4 cup	3/4 cup
1/2 cup	1/8 cup + 2 tsp	1/2 cup
1/3 cup	1 TBS + 2 1/2 tsp	1/3 cup
1/4 cup	1 TBS + 1 tsp	1/4 cup
1 TBS	1 tsp	1 TBS
1 1/2 tsp	1/2 tsp	1 1/2 tsp
1 tsp	1/4 tsp	1 tsp

1 cup green beans + 3 cups water = 3 cups green beans

Green Peas, Dehydrated

Amount	Product	Water
1 cup	1/2 cup	1 cup
3/4 cup	3/8 cup	3/4 cup
1/2 cup	1/4 cup	1/2 cup
1/3 cup	1/8 cup + 2 tsp	1/3 cup
1/4 cup	1/8 cup	1/4 cup
1 TBS	1 1/2 tsp	1 TBS
1 1/2 tsp	1 tsp	1 1/2 tsp
1 tsp	1/2 tsp	1 tsp

1 cup green peas + 2 cups water = 2 cups green peas

Green Peas, Freeze-Dried

Amount	Product	Water
1 cup	1/2 cup	1 cup
3/4 cup	3/8 cup	3/4 cup
1/2 cup	1/4 cup	1/2 cup
1/3 cup	1/8 cup + 2 tsp	1/3 cup
1/4 cup	1/8 cup	1/4 cup
1 TBS	1 1/2 tsp	1 TBS
1 1/2 tsp	1 tsp	1 1/2 tsp
1 tsp	1/2 tsp	1 tsp

1/2 cup green peas + 1 cup water = 1 cup green peas

Jalapeno Dices, Dehydrated

Amount	Product	Water
1 cup	3/8 cup + 1 tsp	3/4 cup + 2 1/2 tsp
3/4 cup	1/4 cup + 2 1/2 tsp	1/2 cup + 5 tsp
1/2 cup	1/8 cup + 4 tsp	3/8 cup + 1 tsp
1/3 cup	1/8 cup + 1/2 tsp	1/4 cup + 1 tsp
1/4 cup	1 TBS + 2 tsp	1/8 cup + 4 tsp
1 TBS	1 1/4 tsp	2 1/2 tsp
1 1/2 tsp	1 tsp	1 1/4 tsp
1 tsp	1/2 tsp	1 tsp

1 cup jalapeno + 2 cups water = 2 1/2 cups jalapeno

Leeks, Dehydrated

Amount	Product	Water
1 cup	3/4 cup + 2 1/2 tsp	1 1/2 cups + 5 tsp
3/4 cup	1/2 cup + 5 tsp	1 1/8 cups + 4 tsp
1/2 cup	3/8 cup + 1 tsp	3/4 cup + 2 1/2 tsp
1/3 cup	1/4 cup + 1 tsp	1/2 cup + 2 tsp
1/4 cup	1/8 cup + 4 tsp	3/8 cup + 1 tsp
1 TBS	2 1/2 tsp	1 TBS + 2 tsp
1 1/2 tsp	1 1/4 tsp	2 1/2 tsp
1 tsp	1 tsp	2 tsp

1 cup leeks + 2 cups water = 1 1/4 cups leeks

Mushrooms, Dehydrated

Amount	Product	Water
1 cup	1 cup	2 cups
3/4 cup	3/4 cup	1 1/2 cups
1/2 cup	1/2 cup	1 cup
1/3 cup	1/3 cup	2/3 cup
1/4 cup	1/4 cup	1/2 cup
1 TBS	1 TBS	1/8 cup
1 1/2 tsp	1 1/2 tsp	1 TBS
1 tsp	1 tsp	2 tsp

1 cup mushrooms + 2 cups water = 1 cup mushrooms

Mushrooms, Freeze-Dried

Amount	Product	Water
1 cup	1 cup	2 cups
3/4 cup	3/4 cup	1 1/2 cups
1/2 cup	1/2 cup	1 cup
1/3 cup	1/3 cup	2/3 cup
1/4 cup	1/4 cup	1/2 cup
1 TBS	1 TBS	1/8 cup
1 1/2 tsp	1 1/2 tsp	1 TBS
1 tsp	1 tsp	2 tsp

1 cup mushrooms + 2 cups water = 1 cup mushrooms

Mushrooms, Shiitake, Dehydrated

Amount	Product	Water
1 cup	1 cup	2 cups
3/4 cup	3/4 cup	1 1/2 cups
1/2 cup	1/2 cup	1 cup
1/3 cup	1/3 cup	2/3 cup
1/4 cup	1/4 cup	1/2 cup
1 TBS	1 TBS	1/8 cup
1 1/2 tsp	1 1/2 tsp	1 TBS
1 tsp	1 tsp	2 tsp

1 cup Shiitake mushrooms + 2 cups water = 1 cup Shiitake mushrooms

Okra, Freeze-Dried

Amount	Product	Water
1 cup	1 cup	2 cups
3/4 cup	3/4 cup	1 1/2 cups
1/2 cup	1/2 cup	1 cup
1/3 cup	1/3 cup	2/3 cup
1/4 cup	1/4 cup	1/2 cup
1 TBS	1 TBS	1/8 cup
1 1/2 tsp	1 1/2 tsp	1 TBS
1 tsp	1 tsp	2 tsp

1 cup okra + 2 cups water = 1 cup okra

Onions, Dehydrated

Amount	Product	Water
1 cup	1/3 cup	2/3 cup
3/4 cup	1/4 cup	1/2 cup
1/2 cup	1/8 cup + 2 tsp	1/3 cup
1/3 cup	1 TBS + 2 1/2 tsp	3 TBS + 2 tsp
1/4 cup	1 TBS + 1 tsp	1/8 cup + 2 tsp
1 TBS	1 tsp	2 tsp
1 1/2 tsp	1/2 tsp	1 tsp
1 tsp	1/4 tsp	3/4 tsp

1 cup onions + 2 cups water = 3 cups onions

Onions, Freeze-Dried

Amount	Product	Water
1 cup	1 cup	3 cups
3/4 cup	3/4 cup	2 1/4 cups
1/2 cup	1/2 cup	1 1/2 cups
1/3 cup	1/3 cup	1 cup
1/4 cup	1/4 cup	3/4 cup
1 TBS	1 TBS	1/8 cup + 1 TBS
1 1/2 tsp	1 1/2 tsp	1 TBS + 1 1/2 tsp
1 tsp	1 tsp	1 TBS

4 tsp onions + 1/4 cup water = 4 tsp onions

Diced Potatoes, Dehydrated

Amount	Product	Water
1 cup	1/2 cup	1 cup
3/4 cup	3/8 cup	3/4 cup
1/2 cup	1/4 cup	1/2 cup
1/3 cup	1/8 cup + 2 tsp	1/3 cup
1/4 cup	1/8 cup	1/4 cup
1 TBS	1 1/2 tsp	1 TBS
1 1/2 tsp	1 tsp	1 1/2 tsp
1 tsp	1/2 tsp	1 tsp

1 cup diced potatoes + 2 cups water = 2 cups potatoes

Diced Potatoes, Freeze-Dried

Amount	Product	Water
1 cup	1 cup	2 cups
3/4 cup	3/4 cup	1 1/2 cups
1/2 cup	1/2 cup	1 cup
1/3 cup	1/3 cup	2/3 cup
1/4 cup	1/4 cup	1/2 cup
1 TBS	1 TBS	1/8 cup
1 1/2 tsp	1 1/2 tsp	1 TBS
1 tsp	1 tsp	2 tsp

1 cup diced potatoes + 2 cups water = 1 cup potatoes

Potato Flakes, Dehydrated

Amount	Product	Water (or Milk)
1 cup	2/3 cup	7/8 cup + 1 tsp
3/4 cup	1/2 cup	2/3 cup
1/2 cup	1/3 cup	3/8 cup + 3 1/2 tsp
1/3 cup	3 TBS + 2 tsp	1/4 cup + 2 tsp
1/4 cup	2 TBS + 2 tsp	1/4 cup
1 TBS	2 tsp	1 TBS
1 1/2 tsp	1 tsp	1 1/2 tsp
1 tsp	3/4 tsp	1 tsp

2 cups potatoes + 2 2/3 cups water (or milk) = 3 cups potatoes

Sliced Potatoes, Dehydrated

Amount	Product	Water
1 cup	1/2 cup	1 cup
3/4 cup	3/8 cup	3/4 cup
1/2 cup	1/4 cup	1/2 cup
1/3 cup	1/8 cup + 2 tsp	1/3 cup
1/4 cup	1/8 cup	1/4 cup
1 TBS	1 1/2 tsp	1 TBS
1 1/2 tsp	1 tsp	1 1/2 tsp
1 tsp	1/2 tsp	1 tsp

1 cup sliced potatoes + 2 cups water = 2 cups potatoes

Hash Brown Potatoes, Dehydrated

Amount	Product	Water
1 cup	1/3 cup	1 1/3 cups
3/4 cup	1/4 cup	1 cup
1/2 cup	1/8 cup + 2 tsp	2/3 cup
1/3 cup	1 TBS + 2 1/2 tsp	3/8 cup + 3 1/2 tsp
1/4 cup	1 TBS + 1 tsp	1/2 cup
1 TBS	1 tsp	1 TBS + 1 tsp
1 1/2 tsp	1/2 tsp	2 tsp
1 tsp	1/4 tsp	1 1/2 tsp

1/2 cup hash brown potatoes + 2 cups water = 1 1/2 cups hash brown potatoes

Pumpkin Powder, Dehydrated

Amount	Product	Water
1 cup	1/8 cup + 2 tsp	3/4 cup + 4 tsp
3/4 cup	2 TBS	1/2 cup + 2 TBS
1/2 cup	1 TBS + 1 tsp	3/8 cup + 2 tsp
1/3 cup	1 TBS	1/4 cup + 1 1/2 tsp
1/4 cup	2 tsp	1/8 cup + 4 tsp
1 TBS	1/2 tsp	2 1/2 tsp
1 1/2 tsp	1/4 tsp	1 1/4 tsp
1 tsp	1/8 tsp	1 tsp

1 cup pumpkin powder + 5 cups water = 6 cups pumpkin puree

Shallots, Dehydrated

Amount	Product	Water
1 cup	1/3 cup	2/3 cup
3/4 cup	1/4 cup	1/2 cup
1/2 cup	1/8 cup + 2 tsp	1/3 cup
1/3 cup	1 TBS + 2 1/2 tsp	3 TBS + 2 tsp
1/4 cup	1 TBS + 1 tsp	2 TBS + 2 tsp
1 TBS	1 tsp	2 tsp
1 1/2 tsp	1/2 tsp	1 tsp
1 tsp	1/4 tsp	3/4 tsp

1 cup shallots + 2 cups water = 3 cups shallots

Sweet Peas, Dehydrated

Amount	Product	Water
1 cup	1/2 cup	1 cup
3/4 cup	3/8 cup	3/4 cup
1/2 cup	1/4 cup	1/2 cup
1/3 cup	1/8 cup + 2 tsp	1/3 cup
1/4 cup	1/8 cup	1/4 cup
1 TBS	1 1/2 tsp	1 TBS
1 1/2 tsp	3/4 tsp	1 1/2 tsp
1 tsp	1/2 tsp	1 tsp

1 cup sweet peas + 2 cups water = 2 cups sweet peas

Sweet Potato Powder, Dehydrated

Amount	Product	Water
1 cup	1 cup	1 cup
3/4 cup	3/4 cup	3/4 cup
1/2 cup	1/2 cup	1/2 cup
1/3 cup	1/3 cup	1/3 cup
1/4 cup	1/4 cup	1/4 cup
1 TBS	1 TBS	1 TBS
1 1/2 tsp	1 1/2 tsp	1 1/2 tsp
1 tsp	1 tsp	1 tsp

1 cup sweet potato powder + 1 cup water = 1 cup sweet potato puree

Sweet Potatoes, Dehydrated

Amount	Product	Water
1 cup	1/2 cup	1 cup
3/4 cup	3/8 cup	3/4 cup
1/2 cup	1/4 cup	1/2 cup
1/3 cup	1/8 cup + 2 tsp	1/3 cup
1/4 cup	1/8 cup	1/4 cup
1 TBS	1 1/2 tsp	1 TBS
1 1/2 tsp	3/4 tsp	1 1/2 tsp
1 tsp	1/2 tsp	1 tsp

1 cup sweet potatoes + 2 cups water = 2 cups sweet potatoes

Sweet Potatoes, Freeze-Dried

Amount	Product	Water
1 cup	1 cup	2 cups
3/4 cup	3/4 cup	1 1/2 cups
1/2 cup	1/2 cup	1 cup
1/3 cup	1/3 cup	2/3 cup
1/4 cup	1/4 cup	1/2 cup
1 TBS	1 TBS	1/8 cup
1 1/2 tsp	1 1/2 tsp	1 TBS
1 tsp	1 tsp	2 tsp

1 cup sweet potatoes + 2 cups water = 1 cup sweet potatoes

Spinach, Dehydrated

Amount	Product	Water
1 cup	2/3 cup	1 1/3 cups
3/4 cup	1/2 cup	1 cup
1/2 cup	1/3 cup	2/3 cup
1/3 cup	3 TBS + 2 tsp	3/8 cup + 3 1/2 tsp
1/4 cup	2 TBS + 2 tsp	1/2 cup
1 TBS	2 tsp	1 TBS + 1 tsp
1 1/2 tsp	1 tsp	2 tsp
1 tsp	3/4 tsp	1 1/2 tsp

1 cup spinach + 2 cups water = 1 1/2 cups spinach

Spinach, Freeze-Dried

Amount	Product	Water
1 cup	1 cup	2 cups
3/4 cup	3/4 cup	1 1/2 cups
1/2 cup	1/2 cup	1 cup
1/3 cup	1/3 cup	2/3 cup
1/4 cup	1/4 cup	1/2 cup
1 TBS	1 TBS	1/8 cup
1 1/2 tsp	1 1/2 tsp	1 TBS
1 tsp	1 tsp	2 tsp

1 cup spinach + 2 cups water = 1 cup spinach

Tomato Dices, Dehydrated

Amount	Product	Water
1 cup	1/8 cup + 4 tsp	3/4 cup + 2 1/2 tsp
3/4 cup	1/8 cup + 1 tsp	1/2 cup + 5 tsp
1/2 cup	1 TBS + 2 tsp	3/8 cup + 1 tsp
1/3 cup	1 TBS	1/4 cup + 1 tsp
1/4 cup	2 1/2 tsp	1/8 cup + 4 tsp
1 TBS	1 tsp	2 1/2 tsp
1 1/2 tsp	1/2 tsp	1 1/4 tsp
1 tsp	1/4 tsp	1 tsp

1 cup tomato dices + 4 cups water = 5 cups tomatoes

Tomato Dices, Freeze-Dried

Amount	Product	Water
1 cup	1 cup	1 2/3 cups
3/4 cup	3/4 cup	1 1/4 cups
1/2 cup	1/2 cup	3/4 cup + 4 tsp
1/3 cup	1/3 cup	1/2 cup + 1 TBS
1/4 cup	1/4 cup	3/8 cup + 2 tsp
1 TBS	1 TBS	1 TBS + 2 tsp
1 1/2 tsp	1 1/2 tsp	2 1/2 tsp
1 tsp	1 tsp	2 tsp

2/3 cup tomato dices + 1 cup water = 2/3 cup tomatoes

Tomato Powder – Paste, Dehydrated

Amount	Product	Water
1 cup	3/8 cup + 1 tsp	3/4 cup + 2 1/2 tsp
3/4 cup	1/4 cup + 2 1/2 tsp	1/2 cup + 5 tsp
1/2 cup	1/8 cup + 4 tsp	3/8 cup + 1 tsp
1/3 cup	1/8 cup + 1/2 tsp	1/4 cup + 1 tsp
1/4 cup	1 TBS + 2 tsp	1/8 cup + 4 tsp
1 TBS	1 1/4 tsp	2 1/2 tsp
1 1/2 tsp	1 tsp	1 1/4 tsp
1 tsp	1/2 tsp	1 tsp

1 cup tomato powder + 2 cups water = 2 1/2 cups tomato paste

Tomato Powder – Sauce, Dehydrated

Amount	Product	Water
1 cup	1/8 cup + 4 tsp	3/4 cup + 2 1/2 tsp
3/4 cup	1/8 cup + 1 tsp	1/2 cup + 5 tsp
1/2 cup	1 TBS + 2 tsp	3/8 cup + 1 tsp
1/3 cup	1/8 cup + 1/2 tsp	1/4 cup + 1 tsp
1/4 cup	2 1/2 tsp	1/8 cup + 4 tsp
1 TBS	1 tsp	2 1/2 tsp
1 1/2 tsp	1/2 tsp	1 1/4 tsp
1 tsp	1/4 tsp	1 tsp

1 cup tomato powder + 4 cups water = 5 cups tomato sauce

Vegetable Soup Mix, Dehydrated

Amount	Product	Water
1 cup	1/4 cup	1 cup
3/4 cup	1/8 cup + 1 TBS	3/4 cup
1/2 cup	1/8 cup	1/2 cup
1/3 cup	1 TBS + 1 tsp	1/3 cup
1/4 cup	1 TBS	1/4 cup
1 TBS	1 tsp	1 TBS
1 1/2 tsp	1/2 tsp	1 1/2 tsp
1 tsp	1/4 tsp	1 tsp

1/2 cup vegetable soup mix + 2 cups water = 2 cups vegetable soup

Zucchini, Dehydrated

Amount	Product	Water
1 cup	3/8 cup + 1 tsp	3/4 cup + 2 1/2 tsp
3/4 cup	1/4 cup + 2 1/2 tsp	1/2 cup + 5 tsp
1/2 cup	1/8 cup + 4 tsp	3/8 cup + 1 tsp
1/3 cup	1/8 cup + 1/2 tsp	1/4 cup + 1 tsp
1/4 cup	1 TBS + 2 tsp	1/8 cup + 4 tsp
1 TBS	1 1/4 tsp	2 1/2 tsp
1 1/2 tsp	1 tsp	1 1/4 tsp
1 tsp	1/2 tsp	1 tsp

1 cup zucchini + 2 cups water = 2 1/2 cups zucchini

Zucchini, Freeze-Dried

Amount	Product	Water
1 cup	1 cup	2 cups
3/4 cup	3/4 cup	1 1/2 cups
1/2 cup	1/2 cup	1 cup
1/3 cup	1/3 cup	2/3 cup
1/4 cup	1/4 cup	1/2 cup
1 TBS	1 TBS	1/8 cup
1 1/2 tsp	1 1/2 tsp	1 TBS
1 tsp	1 tsp	2 tsp

1 cup zucchini + 2 cups water = 1 cup zucchini

Fruits

Apple Dices, Freeze-Dried

Amount	Product	Water
1 cup	1 cup	1 cup
3/4 cup	3/4 cup	3/4 cup
1/2 cup	1/2 cup	1/2 cup
1/3 cup	1/3 cup	1/3 cup
1/4 cup	1/4 cup	1/4 cup
1 TBS	1 TBS	1 TBS
1 1/2 tsp	1 1/2 tsp	1 1/2 tsp
1 tsp	1 tsp	1 tsp

1 cup apple dices + 1 cup water = 1 cup apple dices

Apricot, Freeze-Dried

Amount	Product	Water
1 cup	1 cup	1 cup
3/4 cup	3/4 cup	3/4 cup
1/2 cup	1/2 cup	1/2 cup
1/3 cup	1/3 cup	1/3 cup
1/4 cup	1/4 cup	1/4 cup
1 TBS	1 TBS	1 TBS
1 1/2 tsp	1 1/2 tsp	1 1/2 tsp
1 tsp	1 tsp	1 tsp

1 cup apricot + 1 cup water = 1 cup apricot

Banana Slices, Freeze-Dried

Amount	Product	Water
1 cup	1 cup	1 cup
3/4 cup	3/4 cup	3/4 cup
1/2 cup	1/2 cup	1/2 cup
1/3 cup	1/3 cup	1/3 cup
1/4 cup	1/4 cup	1/4 cup
1 TBS	1 TBS	1 TBS
1 1/2 tsp	1 1/2 tsp	1 1/2 tsp
1 tsp	1 tsp	1 tsp

1 cup banana slices + 1 cup water = 1 cup banana slices

Cherries, Freeze-Dried

Amount	Product	Water
1 cup	1 cup	1 cup
3/4 cup	3/4 cup	3/4 cup
1/2 cup	1/2 cup	1/2 cup
1/3 cup	1/3 cup	1/3 cup
1/4 cup	1/4 cup	1/4 cup
1 TBS	1 TBS	1 TBS
1 1/2 tsp	1 1/2 tsp	1 1/2 tsp
1 tsp	1 tsp	1 tsp

1 cup cherries + 1 cup water = 1 cup cherries

Mango, Freeze-Dried

Amount	Product	Water
1 cup	1 cup	1 cup
3/4 cup	3/4 cup	3/4 cup
1/2 cup	1/2 cup	1/2 cup
1/3 cup	1/3 cup	1/3 cup
1/4 cup	1/4 cup	1/4 cup
1 TBS	1 TBS	1 TBS
1 1/2 tsp	1 1/2 tsp	1 1/2 tsp
1 tsp	1 tsp	1 tsp

1 cup mango + 1 cup water = 1 cup mango

Papaya, Freeze-Dried

Amount	Product	Water
1 cup	1 cup	1 cup
3/4 cup	3/4 cup	3/4 cup
1/2 cup	1/2 cup	1/2 cup
1/3 cup	1/3 cup	1/3 cup
1/4 cup	1/4 cup	1/4 cup
1 TBS	1 TBS	1 TBS
1 1/2 tsp	1 1/2 tsp	1 1/2 tsp
1 tsp	1 tsp	1 tsp

1 cup papaya + 1 cup water = 1 cup papaya

Pineapple, Freeze-Dried

Amount	Product	Water
1 cup	1 cup	1 cup
3/4 cup	3/4 cup	3/4 cup
1/2 cup	1/2 cup	1/2 cup
1/3 cup	1/3 cup	1/3 cup
1/4 cup	1/4 cup	1/4 cup
1 TBS	1 TBS	1 TBS
1 1/2 tsp	1 1/2 tsp	1 1/2 tsp
1 tsp	1 tsp	1 tsp

1 cup pineapple + 1 cup water = 1 cup pineapple

Strawberries, Freeze-Dried

Amount	Product	Water
1 cup	1 cup	1 cup
3/4 cup	3/4 cup	3/4 cup
1/2 cup	1/2 cup	1/2 cup
1/3 cup	1/3 cup	1/3 cup
1/4 cup	1/4 cup	1/4 cup
1 TBS	1 TBS	1 TBS
1 1/2 tsp	1 1/2 tsp	1 1/2 tsp
1 tsp	1 tsp	1 tsp

1 cup strawberries + 1 cup water = 1 cup strawberries

Blueberries, Freeze-Dried

Amount	Product	Water
1 cup	1 cup	1 cup
3/4 cup	3/4 cup	3/4 cup
1/2 cup	1/2 cup	1/2 cup
1/3 cup	1/3 cup	1/3 cup
1/4 cup	1/4 cup	1/4 cup
1 TBS	1 TBS	1 TBS
1 1/2 tsp	1 1/2 tsp	1 1/2 tsp
1 tsp	1 tsp	1 tsp

1 cup blueberries + 1 cup water = 1 cup blueberries

Raspberries, Freeze-Dried

Amount	Product	Water
1 cup	1 cup	1 cup
3/4 cup	3/4 cup	3/4 cup
1/2 cup	1/2 cup	1/2 cup
1/3 cup	1/3 cup	1/3 cup
1/4 cup	1/4 cup	1/4 cup
1 TBS	1 TBS	1 TBS
1 1/2 tsp	1 1/2 tsp	1 1/2 tsp
1 tsp	1 tsp	1 tsp

1 cup raspberries + 1 cup water = 1 cup raspberries

Blackberries, Freeze-Dried

Amount	Product	Water
1 cup	1 cup	1 cup
3/4 cup	3/4 cup	3/4 cup
1/2 cup	1/2 cup	1/2 cup
1/3 cup	1/3 cup	1/3 cup
1/4 cup	1/4 cup	1/4 cup
1 TBS	1 TBS	1 TBS
1 1/2 tsp	1 1/2 tsp	1 1/2 tsp
1 tsp	1 tsp	1 tsp

1 cup blackberries + 1 cup water = 1 cup blackberries

Mixed Berries, Freeze-Dried

Amount	Product	Water
1 cup	1 cup	1 cup
3/4 cup	3/4 cup	3/4 cup
1/2 cup	1/2 cup	1/2 cup
1/3 cup	1/3 cup	1/3 cup
1/4 cup	1/4 cup	1/4 cup
1 TBS	1 TBS	1 TBS
1 1/2 tsp	1 1/2 tsp	1 1/2 tsp
1 tsp	1 tsp	1 tsp

1 cup mixed berries + 1 cup water = 1 cup mixed berries

Orange Slices, Freeze-Dried

Amount	Product	Water
1 cup	1 cup	1 cup
3/4 cup	3/4 cup	3/4 cup
1/2 cup	1/2 cup	1/2 cup
1/3 cup	1/3 cup	1/3 cup
1/4 cup	1/4 cup	1/4 cup
1 TBS	1 TBS	1 TBS
1 1/2 tsp	1 1/2 tsp	1 1/2 tsp
1 tsp	1 tsp	1 tsp

1 cup orange slices + 1 cup water = 1 cup orange slices

Pears, Freeze-Dried

Amount	Product	Water
1 cup	1 cup	1 cup
3/4 cup	3/4 cup	3/4 cup
1/2 cup	1/2 cup	1/2 cup
1/3 cup	1/3 cup	1/3 cup
1/4 cup	1/4 cup	1/4 cup
1 TBS	1 TBS	1 TBS
1 1/2 tsp	1 1/2 tsp	1 1/2 tsp
1 tsp	1 tsp	1 tsp

1 cup pears + 1 cup water = 1 cup pears

Peaches, Freeze-Dried

Amount	Product	Water
1 cup	1 cup	1 cup
3/4 cup	3/4 cup	3/4 cup
1/2 cup	1/2 cup	1/2 cup
1/3 cup	1/3 cup	1/3 cup
1/4 cup	1/4 cup	1/4 cup
1 TBS	1 TBS	1 TBS
1 1/2 tsp	1 1/2 tsp	1 1/2 tsp
1 tsp	1 tsp	1 tsp

1 cup peaches + 1 cup water = 1 cup peaches

Raisins, Freeze-Dried

Amount	Product	Water
1 cup	1 cup	1 cup
3/4 cup	3/4 cup	3/4 cup
1/2 cup	1/2 cup	1/2 cup
1/3 cup	1/3 cup	1/3 cup
1/4 cup	1/4 cup	1/4 cup
1 TBS	1 TBS	1 TBS
1 1/2 tsp	1 1/2 tsp	1 1/2 tsp
1 tsp	1 tsp	1 tsp

1 cup raisins + 1 cup water = 1 cup raisins

Dehydrated Beans & Legumes

Black Beans, Dehydrated

Amount	Product	Water
1 cup	1/2 cup	1/2 cup
3/4 cup	3/8 cup	3/8 cup
1/2 cup	1/4 cup	1/4 cup
1/3 cup	1/8 cup + 2 tsp	1/8 cup + 2 tsp
1/4 cup	1/8 cup	1/8 cup
1 TBS	1 1/2 tsp	1 1/2 tsp
1 1/2 tsp	1 tsp	1 tsp
1 tsp	1/2 tsp	1/2 tsp

1 cup black beans + 1 cup water = 2 cups black beans

Dark Kidney Beans, Dehydrated

Amount	Product	Water
1 cup	1/2 cup	1/2 cup
3/4 cup	3/8 cup	3/8 cup
1/2 cup	1/4 cup	1/4 cup
1/3 cup	1/8 cup + 2 tsp	1/8 cup + 2 tsp
1/4 cup	1/8 cup	1/8 cup
1 TBS	1 1/2 tsp	1 1/2 tsp
1 1/2 tsp	1 tsp	1 tsp
1 tsp	1/2 tsp	1/2 tsp

1 cup dark kidney beans + 1 cup water = 2 cups dark kidney beans

Garbanzo Beans, Dehydrated

Amount	Product	Water
1 cup	1/2 cup	1/2 cup
3/4 cup	3/8 cup	3/8 cup
1/2 cup	1/4 cup	1/4 cup
1/3 cup	1/8 cup + 2 tsp	1/8 cup + 2 tsp
1/4 cup	1/8 cup	1/8 cup
1 TBS	1 1/2 tsp	1 1/2 tsp
1 1/2 tsp	1 tsp	1 tsp
1 tsp	1/2 tsp	1/2 tsp

1 cup garbanzo beans + 1 cup water = 2 cups garbanzo beans

Great Northern Beans, Dehydrated

Amount	Product	Water
1 cup	1/2 cup	1/2 cup
3/4 cup	3/8 cup	3/8 cup
1/2 cup	1/4 cup	1/4 cup
1/3 cup	1/8 cup + 2 tsp	1/8 cup + 2 tsp
1/4 cup	1/8 cup	1/8 cup
1 TBS	1 1/2 tsp	1 1/2 tsp
1 1/2 tsp	1 tsp	1 tsp
1 tsp	1/2 tsp	1/2 tsp

1 cup great northern beans + 1 cup water = 2 cups great northern beans

Lentils, Dehydrated

Amount	Product	Water
1 cup	1/2 cup	1/2 cup
3/4 cup	3/8 cup	3/8 cup
1/2 cup	1/4 cup	1/4 cup
1/3 cup	1/8 cup + 2 tsp	1/8 cup + 2 tsp
1/4 cup	1/8 cup	1/8 cup
1 TBS	1 1/2 tsp	1 1/2 tsp
1 1/2 tsp	1 tsp	1 tsp
1 tsp	1/2 tsp	1/2 tsp

1 cup lentils + 1 cup water = 2 cups lentils

Navy Beans, Dehydrated

Amount	Product	Water
1 cup	1/2 cup	1/2 cup
3/4 cup	3/8 cup	3/8 cup
1/2 cup	1/4 cup	1/4 cup
1/3 cup	1/8 cup + 2 tsp	1/8 cup + 2 tsp
1/4 cup	1/8 cup	1/8 cup
1 TBS	1 1/2 tsp	1 1/2 tsp
1 1/2 tsp	1 tsp	1 tsp
1 tsp	1/2 tsp	1/2 tsp

1 cup navy beans + 1 cup water = 2 cups navy beans

Pinto Beans, Dehydrated

Amount	Product	Water
1 cup	1/2 cup	1/2 cup
3/4 cup	3/8 cup	3/8 cup
1/2 cup	1/4 cup	1/4 cup
1/3 cup	1/8 cup + 2 tsp	1/8 cup + 2 tsp
1/4 cup	1/8 cup	1/8 cup
1 TBS	1 1/2 tsp	1 1/2 tsp
1 1/2 tsp	1 tsp	1 tsp
1 tsp	1/2 tsp	1/2 tsp

1 cup pinto beans + 1 cup water = 2 cups pinto beans

Red Beans, Dehydrated

Amount	Product	Water
1 cup	1/2 cup	1/2 cup
3/4 cup	3/8 cup	3/8 cup
1/2 cup	1/4 cup	1/4 cup
1/3 cup	1/8 cup + 2 tsp	1/8 cup + 2 tsp
1/4 cup	1/8 cup	1/8 cup
1 TBS	1 1/2 tsp	1 1/2 tsp
1 1/2 tsp	1 tsp	1 tsp
1 tsp	1/2 tsp	1/2 tsp

1 cup red beans + 1 cup water = 2 cups red beans

Split Peas, Dehydrated

Amount	Product	Water
1 cup	1/2 cup	1/2 cup
3/4 cup	3/8 cup	3/8 cup
1/2 cup	1/4 cup	1/4 cup
1/3 cup	1/8 cup + 2 tsp	1/8 cup + 2 tsp
1/4 cup	1/8 cup	1/8 cup
1 TBS	1 1/2 tsp	1 1/2 tsp
1 1/2 tsp	1 tsp	1 tsp
1 tsp	1/2 tsp	1/2 tsp

1 cup split peas + 1 cup water = 2 cups split peas

Dried Beans & Legumes

Beans, Dried

Dried beans are a great source of protein, and like their dehydrated and freeze-dried counterparts, they have a long shelf life. As a general rule, one cup of dried beans will produce three cups of cooked beans.

There are MANY varieties of dried beans including: Adzuki Beans, Anasazi Beans, Appaloosa Beans, Black Beans, Blackeyed Peas, Calypso Beans, Cannellini Beans, Christmas Lima Beans, Cranberry Beans, Dapple Grey Beans, European Soldier Beans, Fava Beans, Flageolet Beans, Garbanzo Beans, Great Northern Beans, Green Split Peas, Habas Beans, Jackson Wonder Beans, Jacobs Cattle Beans, Kidney Beans, Lentils, Lima Beans, Lupini Beans, Marrow Beans, Mayocoba Beans, Moccasin Beans, Mung Beans, Navy Beans, Orca Beans, Peruanao Beans, Pigeon Peas, Pink Beans, Pinto Beans, Provence Beans, Rattlesnake Beans, Rice Beans, Red Beans, Snow Cap Beans, White Emergo Beans, and Yellow Eye Beans.

Unlike dehydrated beans, dried beans need to be pre-soaked prior to cooking. When pre-soaking the beans, cover the beans with two inches of water, and soak for a minimum of two hours. Pour off the soaking water, add fresh water, and cook according to the recipe. The chart below shows the amount of dried beans needed to produce the desired amount of cooked beans.

Cooked Amount		Dried Beans US	Dried Beans Metric (ml)
US	Metric (ml)		
1 cup	237	1/3 cup	79
3/4 cup	178	1/4 cup	59
1/2 cup	118.5	1/8 cup + 2 tsp	55
1/3 cup	79	1 TBS + 2 tsp	27
1/4 cup	59	1 TBS + 1 tsp	20
1 TBS	15	1 tsp	5
1 1/2 tsp	7.5	1/2 tsp	2.5
1 tsp	5	1/3 tsp	1.5

1 cup dried beans = 3 cups cooked beans

Textured Vegetable Protein (TVP)

Bacon Bits, TVP

Amount	Product	Water
1 cup	1 cup	1 cup
3/4 cup	3/4 cup	3/4 cup
1/2 cup	1/2 cup	1/2 cup
1/3 cup	1/3 cup	1/3 cup
1/4 cup	1/4 cup	1/4 cup
1 TBS	1 TBS	1 TBS
1 1/2 tsp	1 1/2 tsp	1 1/2 tsp
1 tsp	1 tsp	1 tsp

1 cup bacon bits TVP + 1 cup water = 1 cup bacon bits

Beef Bits, TVP

Amount	Product	Water
1 cup	1/3 cup	2/3 cup
3/4 cup	1/4 cup	1/2 cup
1/2 cup	1/8 cup + 2 tsp	1/3 cup
1/3 cup	1 TBS + 2 1/2 tsp	3 TBS + 2 tsp
1/4 cup	1 TBS + 1 tsp	1/8 cup + 2 tsp
1 TBS	1 tsp	2 tsp
1 1/2 tsp	1/2 tsp	1 tsp
1 tsp	1/4 tsp	3/4 tsp

1 cup beef bits TVP + 2 cups water = 3 cups beef bits

Beef Chunks, TVP

Amount	Product	Water
1 cup	2/3 cup	1 1/3 cups
3/4 cup	1/2 cup	1 cup
1/2 cup	1/3 cup	2/3 cup
1/3 cup	3 TBS + 2 tsp	3/8 cup + 3 1/2 tsp
1/4 cup	2 TBS + 2 tsp	1/2 cup
1 TBS	2 tsp	1 TBS + 1 tsp
1 1/2 tsp	1 tsp	2 tsp
1 tsp	3/4 tsp	1 1/2 tsp

1 cup beef chunks TVP + 2 cups water = 1 1/2 cups beef chunks

Chicken Bits, TVP

Amount	Product	Water
1 cup	3/8 cup + 1 tsp	3/4 cup + 2 1/2 tsp
3/4 cup	1/4 cup + 2 1/2 tsp	1/2 cup + 5 tsp
1/2 cup	1/8 cup + 4 tsp	3/8 cup + 1 tsp
1/3 cup	1/8 cup + 1/2 tsp	1/4 cup + 1 tsp
1/4 cup	1 TBS + 2 tsp	1/8 cup + 4 tsp
1 TBS	1 1/4 tsp	2 1/2 tsp
1 1/2 tsp	1 tsp	1 1/4 tsp
1 tsp	1/2 tsp	1 tsp

1 cup chicken bits TVP + 2 cups water = 2 1/2 cups chicken bits

Chicken Chunks, TVP

Amount	Product	Water
1 cup	2/3 cup	1 1/3 cups
3/4 cup	1/2 cup	1 cup
1/2 cup	1/3 cup	2/3 cup
1/3 cup	3 TBS + 2 tsp	3/8 cup + 3 1/2 tsp
1/4 cup	2 TBS + 2 tsp	1/2 cup
1 TBS	2 tsp	1 TBS + 1 tsp
1 1/2 tsp	1 tsp	2 tsp
1 tsp	3/4 tsp	1 1/2 tsp

1 cup TVP chicken chunks + 2 cups water = 1 1/2 cups chicken chunks

Ham Bits, TVP

Amount	Product	Water
1 cup	1/2 cup	1 cup
3/4 cup	3/8 cup	3/4 cup
1/2 cup	1/4 cup	1/2 cup
1/3 cup	1/8 cup + 2 tsp	1/3 cup
1/4 cup	1/8 cup	1/4 cup
1 TBS	1 1/2 tsp	1 TBS
1 1/2 tsp	1 tsp	1 1/2 tsp
1 tsp	1/2 tsp	1 tsp

1 cup ham bits TVP + 2 cups water = 2 cups ham bits

Pepperoni, TVP

Amount	Product	Water
1 cup	1 cup	1 cup
3/4 cup	3/4 cup	3/4 cup
1/2 cup	1/2 cup	1/2 cup
1/3 cup	1/3 cup	1/3 cup
1/4 cup	1/4 cup	1/4 cup
1 TBS	1 TBS	1 TBS
1 1/2 tsp	1 1/2 tsp	1 1/2 tsp
1 tsp	1 tsp	1 tsp

1 cup pepperoni TVP + 1 cup water = 1 cup pepperoni

Plain, TVP

Amount	Product	Water
1 cup	3/8 cup + 3 1/2 tsp	3/4 cup + 1/8 cup + 1 tsp
3/4 cup	1/3 cup	2/3 cup
1/2 cup	1/8 cup + 5 tsp	3/8 cup + 3 1/2 tsp
1/3 cup	1/8 cup + 1 tsp	1/4 cup + 2 tsp
1/4 cup	1 TBS + 2 1/2 tsp	1/8 cup + 5 tsp
1 TBS	1 1/2 tsp	1 TBS
1 1/2 tsp	1 tsp	1 1/2 tsp
1 tsp	1/2 tsp	1 tsp

1 cup plain TVP + 2 cups water = 2 1/4 cups TVP

Sausage Bits, TVP

Amount	Product	Water
1 cup	2/3 cup	2/3 cup
3/4 cup	1/2 cup	1/2 cup
1/2 cup	1/3 cup	1/3 cup
1/3 cup	1/8 cup + 5 tsp	1/8 cup + 5 tsp
1/4 cup	1/8 cup + 2 tsp	1/8 cup + 2 tsp
1 TBS	2 tsp	2 tsp
1 1/2 tsp	1 tsp	1 tsp
1 tsp	3/4 tsp	3/4 tsp

2/3 cup sausage bits TVP + 2/3 cup water = 1 cup sausage bits

Sloppy Joe Mix, TVP

Amount	Product	Water
1 cup	1/2 cup	1 cup
3/4 cup	3/8 cup	3/4 cup
1/2 cup	1/4 cup	1/2 cup
1/3 cup	1/8 cup + 2 tsp	1/3 cup
1/4 cup	1/8 cup	1/4 cup
1 TBS	1 1/2 tsp	1 TBS
1 1/2 tsp	1 tsp	1 1/2 tsp
1 tsp	1/2 tsp	1 tsp

1 cup Sloppy Joe mix TVP + 2 cups water = 2 cups Sloppy Joe

Taco Bits, TVP

Amount	Product	Water
1 cup	1/2 cup	1 cup
3/4 cup	3/8 cup	3/4 cup
1/2 cup	1/4 cup	1/2 cup
1/3 cup	1/8 cup + 2 tsp	1/3 cup
1/4 cup	1/8 cup	1/4 cup
1 TBS	1 1/2 tsp	1 TBS
1 1/2 tsp	1 tsp	1 1/2 tsp
1 tsp	1/2 tsp	1 tsp

1 cup taco bits + 2 cups water = 2 cups taco bits

Freeze-Dried Meat

Beef – Ground, Freeze-Dried

Amount	Product	Water
1 cup	1 cup	2 cups
3/4 cup	3/4 cup	1 1/2 cups
1/2 cup	1/2 cup	1 cup
1/3 cup	1/3 cup	2/3 cup
1/4 cup	1/4 cup	1/2 cup
1 TBS	1 TBS	1/8 cup
1 1/2 tsp	1 1/2 tsp	1 TBS
1 tsp	1 tsp	2 tsp

1 cup ground beef + 2 cups water = 1 cup ground beef (drain excess water)

Beef – Roast, Freeze-Dried

Amount	Product	Water
1 cup	1 cup	2 cups
3/4 cup	3/4 cup	1 1/2 cups
1/2 cup	1/2 cup	1 cup
1/3 cup	1/3 cup	2/3 cup
1/4 cup	1/4 cup	1/2 cup
1 TBS	1 TBS	1/8 cup
1 1/2 tsp	1 1/2 tsp	1 TBS
1 tsp	1 tsp	2 tsp

1 cup roast beef + 2 cups water = 1 cup roast beef (drain excess water)

Chicken Dices, Freeze-Dried

Amount	Product	Water
1 cup	1 cup	2 cups
3/4 cup	3/4 cup	1 1/2 cups
1/2 cup	1/2 cup	1 cup
1/3 cup	1/3 cup	2/3 cup
1/4 cup	1/4 cup	1/2 cup
1 TBS	1 TBS	1/8 cup
1 1/2 tsp	1 1/2 tsp	1 TBS
1 tsp	1 tsp	2 tsp

1 cup chicken dices + 2 cups water = 1 cup chicken dices (drain excess water)

Chicken Slices, Freeze-Dried

Amount	Product	Water
1 cup	1 cup	2 cups
3/4 cup	3/4 cup	1 1/2 cups
1/2 cup	1/2 cup	1 cup
1/3 cup	1/3 cup	2/3 cup
1/4 cup	1/4 cup	1/2 cup
1 TBS	1 TBS	1/8 cup
1 1/2 tsp	1 1/2 tsp	1 TBS
1 tsp	1 tsp	2 tsp

1 cup chicken + 2 cups water = 1 cup chicken slices (drain excess water)

Ham Dices, Freeze-Dried

Amount	Product	Water
1 cup	1 cup	2 cups
3/4 cup	3/4 cup	1 1/2 cups
1/2 cup	1/2 cup	1 cup
1/3 cup	1/3 cup	2/3 cup
1/4 cup	1/4 cup	1/2 cup
1 TBS	1 TBS	1/8 cup
1 1/2 tsp	1 1/2 tsp	1 TBS
1 tsp	1 tsp	2 tsp

1 cup ham dices + 2 cups water = 1 cup ham dices (drain excess water)

Meatballs, Freeze-Dried

Amount	Product	Water
1 cup	1 cup	2 cups
3/4 cup	3/4 cup	1 1/2 cups
1/2 cup	1/2 cup	1 cup
1/3 cup	1/3 cup	2/3 cup
1/4 cup	1/4 cup	1/2 cup
1 TBS	1 TBS	1/8 cup
1 1/2 tsp	1 1/2 tsp	1 TBS
1 tsp	1 tsp	2 tsp

1 cup meatballs + 2 cups water = 1 cup meatballs (drain excess water)

Sausage Bits, Freeze-Dried

Amount	Product	Water
1 cup	1 cup	2 cups
3/4 cup	3/4 cup	1 1/2 cups
1/2 cup	1/2 cup	1 cup
1/3 cup	1/3 cup	2/3 cup
1/4 cup	1/4 cup	1/2 cup
1 TBS	1 TBS	1/8 cup
1 1/2 tsp	1 1/2 tsp	1 TBS
1 tsp	1 tsp	2 tsp

1 cup sausage bits + 2 cups water = 1 cup sausage bits (drain excess water)

Turkey, Freeze-Dried

Amount	Product	Water
1 cup	1 cup	2 cups
3/4 cup	3/4 cup	1 1/2 cups
1/2 cup	1/2 cup	1 cup
1/3 cup	1/3 cup	2/3 cup
1/4 cup	1/4 cup	1/2 cup
1 TBS	1 TBS	1/8 cup
1 1/2 tsp	1 1/2 tsp	1 TBS
1 tsp	1 tsp	2 tsp

1 cup turkey + 2 cups water = 1 cup turkey (drain excess water)

Cheeses

Blue Cheese Powder, Cheese Sauce

Amount	Product	Water
1 cup	1/4 cup	1 cup
3/4 cup	1/8 cup + 1 TBS	3/4 cup
1/2 cup	1/8 cup	1/2 cup
1/3 cup	1 TBS + 1 tsp	1/3 cup
1/4 cup	1 TBS	1/4 cup
1 TBS	1 tsp	1 TBS
1 1/2 tsp	1/2 tsp	1 1/2 tsp
1 tsp	1/4 tsp	1 tsp

1/2 cup cheese powder + 2 cups water = 2 cups product

Cheddar Powder, Cheese Sauce

Amount	Product	Water
1 cup	1/4 cup	1 cup
3/4 cup	1/8 cup + 1 TBS	3/4 cup
1/2 cup	1/8 cup	1/2 cup
1/3 cup	1 TBS + 1 tsp	1/3 cup
1/4 cup	1 TBS	1/4 cup
1 TBS	1 tsp	1 TBS
1 1/2 tsp	1/2 tsp	1 1/2 tsp
1 tsp	1/4 tsp	1 tsp

1/2 cup cheese powder + 2 cups water = 2 cups product

Parmesan Cheese Powder, Cheese Sauce

Amount	Product	Water
1 cup	1/4 cup	1 cup
3/4 cup	1/8 cup + 1 TBS	3/4 cup
1/2 cup	1/8 cup	1/2 cup
1/3 cup	1 TBS + 1 tsp	1/3 cup
1/4 cup	1 TBS	1/4 cup
1 TBS	1 tsp	1 TBS
1 1/2 tsp	1/2 tsp	1 1/2 tsp
1 tsp	1/4 tsp	1 tsp

1/2 cup cheese powder + 2 cups water = 2 cups product

White Cheddar Powder, Cheese Sauce

Amount	Product	Water
1 cup	1/4 cup	1 cup
3/4 cup	1/8 cup + 1 TBS	3/4 cup
1/2 cup	1/8 cup	1/2 cup
1/3 cup	1 TBS + 1 tsp	1/3 cup
1/4 cup	1 TBS	1/4 cup
1 TBS	1 tsp	1 TBS
1 1/2 tsp	1/2 tsp	1 1/2 tsp
1 tsp	1/4 tsp	1 tsp

1/2 cup cheese powder + 2 cups water = 2 cups product

Cheddar, Freeze-Dried

Amount	Product	Water
1 cup	1 cup	2 cups
3/4 cup	3/4 cup	1 1/2 cups
1/2 cup	1/2 cup	1 cup
1/3 cup	1/3 cup	2/3 cup
1/4 cup	1/4 cup	1/2 cup
1 TBS	1 TBS	1/8 cup
1 1/2 tsp	1 1/2 tsp	1 TBS
1 tsp	1 tsp	2 tsp

1 cup cheese + 2 cups water = 1 cup product (drain excess water)

Colby, Freeze-Dried

Amount	Product	Water
1 cup	1 cup	1 cup
3/4 cup	3/4 cup	3/4 cup
1/2 cup	1/2 cup	1/2 cup
1/3 cup	1/3 cup	1/3 cup
1/4 cup	1/4 cup	1/4 cup
1 TBS	1 TBS	1 TBS
1 1/2 tsp	1 1/2 tsp	1 1/2 tsp
1 tsp	1 tsp	1 tsp

1 cup cheese + 1 cup water = 1 cup product (drain excess water)

Cottage Cheese, Freeze-Dried

Amount	Product	Water
1 cup	1 cup	2/3 cup
3/4 cup	3/4 cup	1/2 cup
1/2 cup	1/2 cup	1/3 cup
1/3 cup	1/3 cup	3 TBS + 2 tsp
1/4 cup	1/4 cup	2 TBS + 2 tsp
1 TBS	1 TBS	2 tsp
1 1/2 tsp	1 1/2 tsp	1 tsp
1 tsp	1 tsp	3/4 tsp

1/2 cup dry cottage cheese + 1/3 cup water = 1/2 cup product

Monterey Jack, Freeze-Dried

Amount	Product	Water
1 cup	1 cup	1 cup
3/4 cup	3/4 cup	3/4 cup
1/2 cup	1/2 cup	1/2 cup
1/3 cup	1/3 cup	1/3 cup
1/4 cup	1/4 cup	1/4 cup
1 TBS	1 TBS	1 TBS
1 1/2 tsp	1 1/2 tsp	1 1/2 tsp
1 tsp	1 tsp	1 tsp

1 cup cheese + 1 cup water = 1 cup product (drain excess water)

Mozzarella, Freeze-Dried

Amount	Product	Water
1 cup	1 cup	2 cups
3/4 cup	3/4 cup	1 1/2 cups
1/2 cup	1/2 cup	1 cup
1/3 cup	1/3 cup	2/3 cup
1/4 cup	1/4 cup	1/2 cup
1 TBS	1 TBS	1/8 cup
1 1/2 tsp	1 1/2 tsp	1 TBS
1 tsp	1 tsp	2 tsp

1 cup cheese + 1 cup water = 1 cup product (drain excess water)

Eggs & Dairy

Whole Eggs, Powdered

Amount	Product	Water
12 eggs	1 1/2 cups	2 1/4 cups
11 eggs	1 cup + 6 TBS	2 cups + 1 TBS
10 eggs	1 1/4 cups	1 3/4 cup + 2 TBS
9 eggs	1 cup + 2 TBS	1 1/2 cups + 3 TBS
8 eggs	1 cup	1 1/4 cups + 1 TBS
7 eggs	3/4 cup + 2 TBS	1 cup + 5 tsp
6 eggs	3/4 cup	1 cup + 2 TBS
5 eggs	1/2 cup + 2 TBS	3/4 cup + 3 TBS
4 eggs	1/2 cup	3/4 cup
3 eggs	6 TBS	3 TBS
2 eggs	4 TBS	2 TBS
1 egg	2 TBS	3 TBS

1 egg = 2 TBS whole egg powder with 3 TBS of water

Egg Whites, Powdered

Amount	Product	Water
12 eggs	1 1/2 cups	2 1/4 cups
11 eggs	1 cup + 6 TBS	2 cups + 1 TBS
10 eggs	1 1/4 cups	1 7/8 cups
9 eggs	1 cup + 2 TBS	1 1/2 cups + 3 TBS
8 eggs	1 cup	1 1/4 cups + 1 TBS
7 eggs	3/4 cup + 2 TBS	1 cup + 5 tsp
6 eggs	3/4 cup	1 cup + 2 TBS
5 eggs	1/2 cup + 2 TBS	3/4 cup + 3 TBS
4 eggs	1/2 cup	3/4 cup
3 eggs	6 TBS	3 TBS
2 eggs	4 TBS	2 TBS
1 egg	2 TBS	3 TBS

1 egg = 2 TBS egg powder with 2 TBS of water

Sour Cream, Powdered

Amount	Product	Water
1 cup	1/4 cup	1 cup
3/4 cup	3 TBS	3/4 cup
1/2 cup	2 TBS	1/2 cup
1/3 cup	4 tsp	1/3 cup
1/4 cup	1 TBS	1/4 cup
1 TBS	3/4 tsp	1 TBS
1 1/2 tsp	1/3 tsp	1 1/2 tsp
1 tsp	1/4 tsp	1 tsp

1/4 cup sour cream powder + 1 cup water = 1 cup sour cream

Buttermilk, Powdered

Amount	Product	Water
1 cup	1/3 cup	1 cup
3/4 cup	1/4 cup	3/4 cup
1/2 cup	2 TBS + 2 tsp	1/2 cup
1/3 cup	5 1/4 tsp	1/3 cup
1/4 cup	4 tsp	1/4 cup
1 TBS	1 tsp	1 TBS
1 1/2 tsp	1/2 tsp	1 1/2 tsp
1 tsp	1/3 tsp	1 tsp

1/3 cup buttermilk powder + 1 cup water = 1 cup buttermilk

Milk, Powdered

Amount	Product	Water
1 cup	1/4 cup	1 cup
3/4 cup	3 TBS	3/4 cup
1/2 cup	2 TBS	1/2 cup
1/3 cup	4 tsp	1/3 cup
1/4 cup	1 TBS	1/4 cup
1 TBS	3/4 tsp	1 TBS
1 1/2 tsp	1/3 tsp	1 1/2 tsp
1 tsp	1/4 tsp	1 tsp

1/4 cup milk powder + 1 cup water = 1 cup milk

Heavy Cream, Powdered

Amount	Product	Water
1 cup	1/3 cup	1 cup
3/4 cup	1/4 cup	3/4 cup
1/2 cup	1/8 cup	1/2 cup
1/3 cup	1 TBS + 2 1/4 tsp	1/3 cup
1/4 cup	1 TBS + 1 tsp	1/4 cup
1 TBS	1 tsp	1 TBS
1 1/2 tsp	1/2 tsp	1 1/2 tsp
1 tsp	1/3 tsp	1 tsp

1/3 cup heavy cream powder + 1 cup water = 1 cup heavy cream

Butter, Powdered

Amount	Product	Water
1 cup	1 cup	7/8 cup
3/4 cup	3/4 cup	1/2 cup
1/2 cup	1/2 cup	2/3 cup
1/3 cup	1/3 cup	2 TBS + 2 tsp
1/4 cup	1/4 cup	3 TBS
1 TBS	1 TBS	2 1/2 tsp
1 1/2 tsp	1 1/2 tsp	1 1/3 tsp
1 tsp	1 tsp	3/4 tsp

1/4 cup + 3 TBS water to 1/2 cup butter powder = 1/2 cup = 1 stick

Margarine, Powdered

Amount	Product	Water
1 cup	1 cup	7/8 cup
3/4 cup	3/4 cup	1/2 cup
1/2 cup	1/2 cup	2/3 cup
1/3 cup	1/3 cup	2 TBS + 2 tsp
1/4 cup	1/4 cup	3 TBS
1 TBS	1 TBS	2 1/2 tsp
1 1/2 tsp	1 1/2 tsp	1 1/3 tsp
1 tsp	1 tsp	3/4 tsp

1/4 cup + 3 TBS water to 1/2 cup margarine powder = 1/2 cup = 1 stick

Cream Cheese, Powdered

Amount	Product	Water
1 cup	1 3/4 cups	1/2 cup
3/4 cup	1 1/4 cups + 1 1/2 tsp	6 TBS
1/2 cup	2/3 cup + 3 TBS	1/4 cup
1/3 cup	1/2 cup + 1 TBS	2 TBS + 2 tsp
1/4 cup	6 TBS + 2 1/2 tsp	2 TBS
1 TBS	5 tsp	1 1/2 tsp
1 1/2 tsp	2 1/2 tsp	3/4 tsp
1 tsp	1 3/4 tsp	1/2 tsp

To make 3 oz. of cream cheese use 10 TBS of cream cheese powder to 3 TBS of water.
To make 8 oz. of cream cheese use 1 3/4 cup cream cheese powder to 1/2 cup of water.

Fruit Powders

Banana, Powdered

Amount	Product	Water
1 cup	3 TBS + 1 2/3 tsp	1 cup
3/4 cup	2 TBS + 1 1/2 tsp	3/4 cup
1/2 cup	5 1/3 tsp	1/2 cup
1/3 cup	3 1/2 tsp	1/3 cup
1/4 cup	2 2/3 tsp	1/4 cup
1 TBS	2/3 tsp	1 TBS
1 1/2 tsp	1/3 tsp	1 1/2 tsp
1 tsp	1/4 tsp	1 tsp

2 tsp banana powder + 3 TBS water = 3 TBS banana juice

Blackberry Juice, Powdered

Amount	Product	Water
1 cup	3 TBS + 1 2/3 tsp	1 cup
3/4 cup	2 TBS + 1 1/2 tsp	3/4 cup
1/2 cup	5 1/3 tsp	1/2 cup
1/3 cup	3 1/2 tsp	1/3 cup
1/4 cup	2 2/3 tsp	1/4 cup
1 TBS	2/3 tsp	1 TBS
1 1/2 tsp	1/3 tsp	1 1/2 tsp
1 tsp	1/4 tsp	1 tsp

2 tsp blackberry powder + 3 TBS water = 3 TBS blackberry juice

Blueberry Juice, Powdered

Amount	Product	Water
1 cup	3 TBS + 1 2/3 tsp	1 cup
3/4 cup	2 TBS + 1 1/2 tsp	3/4 cup
1/2 cup	5 1/3 tsp	1/2 cup
1/3 cup	3 1/2 tsp	1/3 cup
1/4 cup	2 2/3 tsp	1/4 cup
1 TBS	2/3 tsp	1 TBS
1 1/2 tsp	1/3 tsp	1 1/2 tsp
1 tsp	1/4 tsp	1 tsp

2 tsp blueberry powder + 3 TBS water = 3 TBS blueberry juice

Cherry Juice, Powdered

Amount	Product	Water
1 cup	3 TBS + 1 2/3 tsp	1 cup
3/4 cup	2 TBS + 1 1/2 tsp	3/4 cup
1/2 cup	5 1/3 tsp	1/2 cup
1/3 cup	3 1/2 tsp	1/3 cup
1/4 cup	2 2/3 tsp	1/4 cup
1 TBS	2/3 tsp	1 TBS
1 1/2 tsp	1/3 tsp	1 1/2 tsp
1 tsp	1/4 tsp	1 tsp

2 tsp cherry powder + 3 TBS water = 3 TBS cherry juice

Lemon Juice, Powdered

Amount	Product	Water
1 cup	3 TBS + 1 2/3 tsp	1 cup
3/4 cup	2 TBS + 1 1/2 tsp	3/4 cup
1/2 cup	5 1/3 tsp	1/2 cup
1/3 cup	3 1/2 tsp	1/3 cup
1/4 cup	2 2/3 tsp	1/4 cup
1 TBS	2/3 tsp	1 TBS
1 1/2 tsp	1/3 tsp	1 1/2 tsp
1 tsp	1/4 tsp	1 tsp

2 tsp lemon powder + 3 TBS water = 3 TBS lemon juice

Lime Juice, Powdered

Amount	Product	Water
1 cup	3 TBS + 1 2/3 tsp	1 cup
3/4 cup	2 TBS + 1 1/2 tsp	3/4 cup
1/2 cup	5 1/3 tsp	1/2 cup
1/3 cup	3 1/2 tsp	1/3 cup
1/4 cup	2 2/3 tsp	1/4 cup
1 TBS	2/3 tsp	1 TBS
1 1/2 tsp	1/3 tsp	1 1/2 tsp
1 tsp	1/4 tsp	1 tsp

2 tsp lime powder + 3 TBS water = 3 TBS lime juice

Orange Juice, Powdered

Amount	Product	Water
1 cup	3 TBS + 1 2/3 tsp	1 cup
3/4 cup	2 TBS + 1 1/2 tsp	3/4 cup
1/2 cup	5 1/3 tsp	1/2 cup
1/3 cup	3 1/2 tsp	1/3 cup
1/4 cup	2 2/3 tsp	1/4 cup
1 TBS	2/3 tsp	1 TBS
1 1/2 tsp	1/3 tsp	1 1/2 tsp
1 tsp	1/4 tsp	1 tsp

2 tsp orange powder + 3 TBS water = 3 TBS orange juice

Pineapple Juice, Powdered

Amount	Product	Water
1 cup	3 TBS + 1 2/3 tsp	1 cup
3/4 cup	2 TBS + 1 1/2 tsp	3/4 cup
1/2 cup	5 1/3 tsp	1/2 cup
1/3 cup	3 1/2 tsp	1/3 cup
1/4 cup	2 2/3 tsp	1/4 cup
1 TBS	2/3 tsp	1 TBS
1 1/2 tsp	1/3 tsp	1 1/2 tsp
1 tsp	1/4 tsp	1 tsp

2 tsp pineapple powder + 3 TBS water = 3 TBS pineapple juice

Freeze-Dried Raspberry Juice, Powdered

Amount	Product	Water
1 cup	3 TBS + 1 2/3 tsp	1 cup
3/4 cup	2 TBS + 1 1/2 tsp	3/4 cup
1/2 cup	5 1/3 tsp	1/2 cup
1/3 cup	3 1/2 tsp	1/3 cup
1/4 cup	2 2/3 tsp	1/4 cup
1 TBS	2/3 tsp	1 TBS
1 1/2 tsp	1/3 tsp	1 1/2 tsp
1 tsp	1/4 tsp	1 tsp

2 tsp raspberry powder + 3 TBS water = 3 TBS raspberry juice

Freeze-Dried Strawberry Juice, Powdered

Amount	Product	Water
1 cup	3 TBS + 1 2/3 tsp	1 cup
3/4 cup	2 TBS + 1 1/2 tsp	3/4 cup
1/2 cup	5 1/3 tsp	1/2 cup
1/3 cup	3 1/2 tsp	1/3 cup
1/4 cup	2 2/3 tsp	1/4 cup
1 TBS	2/3 tsp	1 TBS
1 1/2 tsp	1/3 tsp	1 1/2 tsp
1 tsp	1/4 tsp	1 tsp

2 tsp strawberry powder + 3 TBS water = 3 TBS strawberry juice

Powders

Honey, Powdered

Amount	Product	Water
1 cup	3 cups	1 cup
3/4 cup	2 1/4 cup	3/4 cup
1/2 cup	1 1/2 cup	1/2 cup
1/3 cup	1 cup	1/3 cup
1/4 cup	3/4 cup	1/4 cup
1 TBS	3 TBS	1 TBS
1 1/2 tsp	1 TBS + 1 1/2 tsp	1 1/2 tsp
1 tsp	1 TBS	1 tsp

3/4 cup honey powder + 1/4 cup water = 1/4 cup honey

Peanut Butter, Powdered

Amount	Product	Water
1 cup	3 cups	2/3 cup
3/4 cup	2 1/4 cup	1/2 cup
1/2 cup	1 1/2 cup	1/3 cup
1/3 cup	1 cup	3 TBS + 1 1/2 tsp
1/4 cup	3/4 cup	2 TBS + 2 tsp
1 TBS	3 TBS	2 tsp
1 1/2 tsp	1 TBS + 1 1/2 tsp	1 tsp
1 tsp	1 TBS	2/3 tsp

2 TBS peanut butter powder + 2 tsp water = 1 TBS (add sugar and oil to taste)

Shortening, Powdered

Amount	Product	Water
1 cup	1 cup	1 cup
3/4 cup	3/4 cup	3/4 cup
1/2 cup	1/2 cup	1/2 cup
1/3 cup	1/3 cup	1/3 cup
1/4 cup	1/4 cup	1/4 cup
1 TBS	1 TBS	1 TBS
1 1/2 tsp	1 1/2 tsp	1 1/2 tsp
1 tsp	1 tsp	1 tsp

1 cup shortening powder + 1 cup water = 1 cup shortening (add oil for texture)

Soy Sauce, Powdered

Amount	Product	Water
1 cup	2/3 cup	1 cup
3/4 cup	1/2 cup	3/4 cup
1/2 cup	1/3 cup	1/2 cup
1/3 cup	3 TBS + 1 1/2 tsp	1/3 cup
1/4 cup	2 TBS + 2 tsp	1/4 cup
1 TBS	2 tsp	1 TBS
1 1/2 tsp	1 tsp	1 1/2 tsp
1 tsp	2/3 tsp	1 tsp

1 tsp soy sauce powder + 1 1/2 tsp water = 1 1/2 tsp soy sauce

Teriyaki Sauce, Powdered

Amount	Product	Water
1 cup	2/3 cup	1 cup
3/4 cup	1/2 cup	3/4 cup
1/2 cup	1/3 cup	1/2 cup
1/3 cup	3 TBS + 1 1/2 tsp	1/3 cup
1/4 cup	2 TBS + 2 tsp	1/4 cup
1 TBS	2 tsp	1 TBS
1 1/2 tsp	1 tsp	1 1/2 tsp
1 tsp	2/3 tsp	1 tsp

1 tsp teriyaki sauce powder + 1 1/2 tsp water = 1 1/2 tsp teriyaki sauce

Vinegar, Powdered

Amount	Product	Water
1 cup	2/3 cup	1 cup
3/4 cup	1/2 cup	3/4 cup
1/2 cup	1/3 cup	1/2 cup
1/3 cup	3 TBS + 1 1/2 tsp	1/3 cup
1/4 cup	2 TBS + 2 tsp	1/4 cup
1 TBS	2 tsp	1 TBS
1 1/2 tsp	1 tsp	1 1/2 tsp
1 tsp	2/3 tsp	1 tsp

1 tsp vinegar powder + 1 1/2 tsp water = 1 1/2 tsp vinegar

Worcestershire Sauce, Powdered

Amount	Product	Water
1 cup	2/3 cup	1 cup
3/4 cup	1/2 cup	3/4 cup
1/2 cup	1/3 cup	1/2 cup
1/3 cup	3 TBS + 1 1/2 tsp	1/3 cup
1/4 cup	2 TBS + 2 tsp	1/4 cup
1 TBS	2 tsp	1 TBS
1 1/2 tsp	1 tsp	1 1/2 tsp
1 tsp	2/3 tsp	1 tsp

1 tsp Worcestershire powder + 1 1/2 tsp water = 1 1/2 tsp Worcestershire sauce

Maple Syrup, Powdered

Amount	Product	Water
1 cup	2 cups	1 cup
3/4 cup	1 1/2 cups	3/4 cup
1/2 cup	1 cup	1/2 cup
1/3 cup	2/3 cup	1/3 cup
1/4 cup	1/2 cup	1/4 cup
1 TBS	2 TBS	1 TBS
1 1/2 tsp	1 TBS	1 1/2 tsp
1 tsp	2 tsp	1 tsp

2 TBS maple syrup powder + 1 TBS water = 1 TBS maple syrup

Wine Powder

Burgundy Wine, Powdered

Amount	Product	Water
1 cup	1 cup	1 cup
3/4 cup	3/4 cup	3/4 cup
1/2 cup	1/2 cup	1/2 cup
1/3 cup	1/3 cup	1/3 cup
1/4 cup	1/4 cup	1/4 cup
1 TBS	1 TBS	1 TBS
1 1/2 tsp	1 1/2 tsp	1 1/2 tsp
1 tsp	1 tsp	1 tsp

1 cup burgundy wine powder + 1 cup water = 1 cup wine

Chablis, Powdered

Amount	Product	Water
1 cup	1 cup	1 cup
3/4 cup	3/4 cup	3/4 cup
1/2 cup	1/2 cup	1/2 cup
1/3 cup	1/3 cup	1/3 cup
1/4 cup	1/4 cup	1/4 cup
1 TBS	1 TBS	1 TBS
1 1/2 tsp	1 1/2 tsp	1 1/2 tsp
1 tsp	1 tsp	1 tsp

1 cup Chablis wine powder + 1 cup water = 1 cup wine

Sherry, Powdered

Amount	Product	Water
1 cup	1 cup	1 cup
3/4 cup	3/4 cup	3/4 cup
1/2 cup	1/2 cup	1/2 cup
1/3 cup	1/3 cup	1/3 cup
1/4 cup	1/4 cup	1/4 cup
1 TBS	1 TBS	1 TBS
1 1/2 tsp	1 1/2 tsp	1 1/2 tsp
1 tsp	1 tsp	1 tsp

1 cup sherry wine powder + 1 cup water = 1 cup wine

PANTRY STUFFERS™
Rehydration Calculations
Made Easy
METRIC MEASUREMENTS
Tables provide dehydrated, freeze-dried & powdered
product substitutions for your favorite recipes
Wanda Bailey Clark

Flip your book over to find
Metric measurements

CPSIA information can be obtained
at www.ICGtesting.com
Printed in the USA
FFOW05n1345180816

9 780983 756163

PANTRY STUFFERS™

Rehydration Calculations Made Easy

METRIC MEASUREMENTS

Wanda Bailey Clark

Pantry Stuffers, LLC
6300 Creedmoor Road
Suite 170, Box 238
Raleigh, NC 27612

Limit of Liability/Disclaimer of Warranty
To the best of our knowledge, the calculations in this book are accurate for ordinary use and users. While Pantry Stuffers, LLC has used its best efforts in preparing this book, it makes no presentations or warranties of merchantability or fitness for a particular purpose. No warranty may be created or extended by sales representatives or written sales materials. The advice and strategies contained herein may not be suitable for your situation. You should consult with a professional where appropriate. Neither the publisher nor Pantry Stuffers, LLC shall be liable for any loss of profit or any other commercial damages, including but not limited to special, incidental, or other damages.

Disclaimer
The measurements within the tables are to be used as a practical guide in calculating how to replace fresh, canned, or frozen products with dehydrated, freeze-dried, dried, or powdered products in your recipes. In some cases, measurements have been rounded up or down slightly to align to standard measurement instruments. Because dehydrated, freeze-dried, and powdered products are organic—the exact amount of water needed for reconstitution may vary slightly based on the amount of water present in the original product prior to processing.

Edited by Edie Mourey www.furrowpress.com

Cover and interior design by David G. Danglis / Pinwheel Creative

Front cover photo: www.istockphoto.com / karimala.
Interior photo: www.istockphoto.com / marilyna.

Printed in the United States of America
Library of Congress Control Number: 2013943204
International Standard Book Number: 978-0-9837561-6-3

Dedication

Every part of this cookbook is dedicated first to Jesus Christ, my Lord and Savior. I pray that this honors Him.

I give honor and appreciation to my husband, Paul, and to my family (David, Bobbie, and Trey) who are my greatest cheerleaders for EVERY project I undertake.

To my beloved friend and business partner, Steve Moore, thank you for handling all of the details behind the scenes and sharing the responsibility for bringing the vision God gave us to reality. To Jen, my friend and Steve's beautiful wife, thank you for all you do to help and encourage both of us through every step of this journey. We wouldn't be here without you!

Table of Recipes

Table of Recipes, cont'd.

Reconstitution

I am a busy suburban wife, mother, and grandmother with a passion for preparedness. While I have always been aware that dehydrated, freeze-dried, and powdered ingredients existed, I only started using them several years ago.

Not only do I package mixes for convenience and disaster support, but I also keep my pantry stuffed with a variety of products that I use to avoid a last-minute trip to the grocery store. Additionally, I maintain a supply to have a nutritious alternative for out-of-season vegetables.

The amount of water needed to reconstitute products is based on how much water was removed during the dehydration, freeze-drying, or powder process. Reconstitution is different product to product.

The purpose of this book is to meet a need I continually experience—especially for last-minute substitutions—how much product and how much water to add!

I hope that this book becomes a valuable tool to you, too, as you incorporate dried products into your pantry!

— Wanda Bailey Clark

The Basics

This book contains rehydration tables for "typical" reconstitution for the products listed. Please note that the reconstitution formula used to calculate the amounts of water and product to add is listed at the bottom of each table. If your product shows a different reconstitution formula, you will need to adjust your calculations.

Dehydration

Dehydration is the oldest, most natural form of food preservation. Ancient civilizations used various forms of open-air drying to dry vegetables and fruits to preserve food for future use. Modern dehydrators use controlled air and heat to effectively remove the moisture content from vegetables and fruits.

Freeze-Drying Process

Freeze-drying is dehydration that works by freezing and then reducing the pressure to allow the frozen water in the material to sublimate directly from the solid phase to the gas phase.

Powder Process

The more you dry a product, the more stable and less susceptible it is to nutritional loss. There are many different processes used to create powdered products. Advances in freeze-drying and spray technologies are constantly adding to the number and variety of powdered food products available. Like the dehydration and freeze-drying processes, food products are powdered when their nutritional value is at its peak.

In addition to fruit and vegetable powders, powdered processes include dairy, syrups, honey, seasonings, and wine.

Nutritional Value

Most vitamins and minerals remain intact during the dehydration process, except for vitamin C which does not tolerate the dehydration process. Dehydration retains more vitamin and mineral content than canned or frozen vegetables. It has also been suggested by many that, in some cases, if the fresh produce in the grocery store has been picked while green and has traveled for days before arriving at the store, then dehydrated vegetables even have a higher vitamin and mineral content than their fresh counterparts.

Measurement Tables

U.S. Measurements

	Teaspoon	Tablespoon	Cup
1 Teaspoon	1	1/3	1/48
1 Tablespoon	3	1	1/16
1/8 cup	6	2	1/8
1/6 cup	8	2 2/3	1/6
1/4 cup	12	4	1/4
1/3 cup	16	5 1/3	1/3
3/8 cup	18	6	3/8
1/2 cup	24	8	1/2
2/3 cup	32	10 2/3	2/3
3/4 cup	36	12	3/4
1 cup	48	16	1

Metric Measurements

US	Metric	Imperial
1/4 teaspoon	1 ml	
1/2 teaspoon	2.5 ml	
1 teaspoon	5 ml	
1 1/2 teaspoon	7.5 ml	
1 Tablespoon	15 ml	
1/8 cup	30 ml	1 fl oz
1/4 cup	59 ml	2 fl oz
1/3 cup	79 ml	2.5 fl oz
1/2 cup	118.5 ml	4 fl oz
2/3 cup	158 ml	5 fl oz
3/4 cup	178 ml	6 fl oz
1 cup	237 ml	8 fl oz
2 cups (1 pint)	474 ml	16 fl oz
1 quart	1 liter	32 fl oz

NOTE: The metric conversion charts within this book are rounded to the nearest 1/2 ml and reference the US rehydration ratios.

Vegetables

Asparagus, Freeze-Dried

Measurements		Product (ml)	Water (ml)
US	Metric		
1 cup	237 ml	237	474
3/4 cup	178 ml	178	356
1/2 cup	118.5 ml	118.5	237
1/3 cup	79 ml	79	158
1/4 cup	59 ml	59	118
1 TBS	15 ml	15	30
1 1/2 tsp	7.5 ml	7.5	15
1 tsp	5 ml	5	10

1 cup asparagus + 2 cups water = 1 cup asparagus

Bell Peppers, Dehydrated

Measurements		Product (ml)	Water (ml)
US	Metric		
1 cup	237 ml	95	190
3/4 cup	178 ml	71	142
1/2 cup	118.5 ml	47	95
1/3 cup	79 ml	32	63
1/4 cup	59 ml	24	47
1 TBS	15 ml	6	12
1 1/2 tsp	7.5 ml	3	6
1 tsp	5 ml	2	4

1 cup peppers + 2 cups water = 2 1/2 cups peppers

Bell Peppers, Freeze-Dried

Measurements		Product (ml)	Water (ml)
US	Metric		
1 cup	237 ml	237	474
3/4 cup	178 ml	178	356
1/2 cup	118.5 ml	118.5	237
1/3 cup	79 ml	79	158
1/4 cup	59 ml	59	118
1 TBS	15 ml	15	30
1 1/2 tsp	7.5 ml	7.5	15
1 tsp	5 ml	5	10

1 cup peppers + 2 cups water = 1 cup peppers

Broccoli, Dehydrated

Measurements		Product (ml)	Water (ml)
US	Metric		
1 cup	237 ml	73	146
3/4 cup	178 ml	55	109.5
1/2 cup	118.5 ml	36.5	73
1/3 cup	79 ml	24.5	49
1/4 cup	59 ml	18	36.5
1 TBS	15 ml	5	9
1 1/2 tsp	7.5 ml	2.5	5
1 tsp	5 ml	1.5	3

1 cup broccoli + 2 cups water = 3 1/4 cups broccoli

Broccoli, Freeze-Dried

Measurements		Product (ml)	Water (ml)
US	Metric		
1 cup	237 ml	118.5	355.5
3/4 cup	178 ml	89	267
1/2 cup	118.5 ml	59	178
1/3 cup	79 ml	39.5	118.5
1/4 cup	59 ml	29.5	88.5
1 TBS	15 ml	7.5	22.5
1 1/2 tsp	7.5 ml	4	11
1 tsp	5 ml	2.5	7.5

1/4 cup broccoli + 3/4 cup water = 1/2 cup broccoli

Cabbage, Dehydrated

Measurements		Product (ml)	Water (ml)
US	Metric		
1 cup	237 ml	68	135.5
3/4 cup	178 ml	51	102
1/2 cup	118.5 ml	34	68
1/3 cup	79 ml	23	45
1/4 cup	59 ml	17	34
1 TBS	15 ml	4.5	9
1 1/2 tsp	7.5 ml	2	4.5
1 tsp	5 ml	1.5	3

1 cup cabbage + 2 cups water = 3 1/2 cups cabbage

Cabbage, Freeze-Dried

Measurements		Product (ml)	Water (ml)
US	Metric		
1 cup	237 ml	118.5	355.5
3/4 cup	178 ml	89	267
1/2 cup	118.5 ml	59	178
1/3 cup	79 ml	39.5	118.5
1/4 cup	59 ml	29.5	88.5
1 TBS	15 ml	7.5	22.5
1 1/2 tsp	7.5 ml	4	11
1 tsp	5 ml	2.5	7.5

1/4 cup cabbage + 3/4 cup water = 1/2 cup cabbage

Carrots, Dehydrated

Measurements		Product (ml)	Water (ml)
US	Metric		
1 cup	237 ml	59	118.5
3/4 cup	178 ml	44.5	89
1/2 cup	118.5 ml	30	59
1/3 cup	79 ml	20	39.5
1/4 cup	59 ml	15	29.5
1 TBS	15 ml	4	7.5
1 1/2 tsp	7.5 ml	2	4
1 tsp	5 ml	1	2.5

1 cup carrots + 2 cups water = 4 cups carrots

Carrots, Freeze-Dried

Measurements		Product (ml)	Water (ml)
US	Metric		
1 cup	237 ml	89	237
3/4 cup	178 ml	67	178
1/2 cup	118.5 ml	44.5	118.5
1/3 cup	79 ml	30	79
1/4 cup	59 ml	22	59
1 TBS	15 ml	6	15
1 1/2 tsp	7.5 ml	3	7.5
1 tsp	5 ml	2	5

3 TBS carrots + 1/2 cups water = 1/2 cup carrots

Cauliflower, Dehydrated

Measurements		Product (ml)	Water (ml)
US	Metric		
1 cup	178 ml	73	146
3/4 cup	118.5 ml	55	109.5
1/2 cup	79 ml	36.5	73
1/3 cup	59 ml	24.5	49
1/4 cup	15 ml	18	36.5
1 TBS	7.5 ml	5	9
1 1/2 tsp	5 ml	2.5	5
1 tsp	237 ml	1.5	3

1 cup cauliflower + 2 cups water = 3 1/4 cups cauliflower

Cauliflower, Freeze-Dried

Measurements		Product (ml)	Water (ml)
US	Metric		
1 cup	237 ml	118.5	355.5
3/4 cup	178 ml	89	267
1/2 cup	118.5 ml	59	178
1/3 cup	79 ml	39.5	118.5
1/4 cup	59 ml	29.5	88.5
1 TBS	15 ml	7.5	22.5
1 1/2 tsp	7.5 ml	4	11
1 tsp	5 ml	2.5	7.5

1/4 cup cauliflower + 3/4 cup water = 1/2 cup cauliflower

Celery, Dehydrated

Measurements		Product (ml)	Water (ml)
US	Metric		
1 cup	237 ml	73	146
3/4 cup	178 ml	55	109.5
1/2 cup	118.5 ml	36.5	73
1/3 cup	79 ml	24.5	49
1/4 cup	59 ml	18	36.5
1 TBS	15 ml	5	9
1 1/2 tsp	7.5 ml	2.5	5
1 tsp	5 ml	1.5	3

1 cup celery + 2 cups water = 3 1/4 cups celery

Celery, Freeze-Dried

Measurements		Product (ml)	Water (ml)
US	Metric		
1 cup	237 ml	237	711
3/4 cup	178 ml	178	534
1/2 cup	118.5 ml	118.5	355.5
1/3 cup	79 ml	79	237
1/4 cup	59 ml	59	177
1 TBS	15 ml	15	45
1 1/2 tsp	7.5 ml	7.5	22.5
1 tsp	5 ml	5	15

1/3 cup celery + 1 cup water = 1/3 cup celery (drain excess water)

Chives, Dehydrated

Measurements		Product (ml)	Water (ml)
US	Metric		
1 cup	237 ml	237	474
3/4 cup	178 ml	178	356
1/2 cup	118.5 ml	118.5	237
1/3 cup	79 ml	79	158
1/4 cup	59 ml	59	118
1 TBS	15 ml	15	30
1 1/2 tsp	7.5 ml	7.5	15
1 tsp	5 ml	5	10

1 cup chives + 2 cups water = 1 cup chives

Chives, Freeze-Dried

Measurements		Product (ml)	Water (ml)
US	Metric		
1 cup	237 ml	237	474
3/4 cup	178 ml	178	356
1/2 cup	118.5 ml	118.5	237
1/3 cup	79 ml	79	158
1/4 cup	59 ml	59	118
1 TBS	15 ml	15	30
1 1/2 tsp	7.5 ml	7.5	15
1 tsp	5 ml	5	10

1 cup chives + 2 cups water = 1 cup chives

Corn, Dehydrated

Measurements		Product (ml)	Water (ml)
US	Metric		
1 cup	237 ml	118.5	237
3/4 cup	178 ml	89	178
1/2 cup	118.5 ml	59	118.5
1/3 cup	79 ml	39.5	79
1/4 cup	59 ml	29.5	59
1 TBS	15 ml	7.5	15
1 1/2 tsp	7.5 ml	4	7.5
1 tsp	5 ml	2.5	5

1 cup corn + 2 cups water = 2 cups corn

Corn, Freeze-Dried

Measurements		Product (ml)	Water (ml)
US	Metric		
1 cup	237 ml	237	474
3/4 cup	178 ml	178	356
1/2 cup	118.5 ml	118.5	237
1/3 cup	79 ml	79	158
1/4 cup	59 ml	59	118
1 TBS	15 ml	15	30
1 1/2 tsp	7.5 ml	7.5	15
1 tsp	5 ml	5	10

1 cup corn + 2 cups water = 1 cup corn

Garlic, Dehydrated

Measurements		Product (ml)	Water (ml)
US	Metric		
1 cup	237 ml	79	158
3/4 cup	178 ml	59.5	119
1/2 cup	118.5 ml	39.5	79
1/3 cup	79 ml	26.5	53
1/4 cup	59 ml	20	39.5
1 TBS	15 ml	5	10
1 1/2 tsp	7.5 ml	2.5	5
1 tsp	5 ml	2	3.5

1 cup garlic + 2 cups water = 3 cups garlic

Garlic Recipe Substitutions for 1 clove of Garlic

Substitution	US Measurement	Metric Measurement
Chopped garlic	1 tsp	5 ml
Minced garlic	1/2 tsp	2.5 ml
Garlic powder	1/8 tsp	1 ml
Garlic flakes	1/2 tsp	2.5 ml
Granulated garlic	1/4 tsp	1 ml
Garlic juice	1/2 tsp	2.5 ml

Green Beans, Dehydrated

Measurements		Product (ml)	Water (ml)
US	Metric		
1 cup	237 ml	79	158
3/4 cup	178 ml	59.5	119
1/2 cup	118.5 ml	39.5	79
1/3 cup	79 ml	26.5	53
1/4 cup	59 ml	20	39.5
1 TBS	15 ml	5	10
1 1/2 tsp	7.5 ml	2.5	5
1 tsp	5 ml	2	3.5

1 cup green beans + 2 cups water = 3 cups green beans

Green Beans, Freeze-Dried

Measurements		Product (ml)	Water (ml)
US	Metric		
1 cup	237 ml	79	237
3/4 cup	178 ml	59.5	178
1/2 cup	118.5 ml	39.5	118.5
1/3 cup	79 ml	26.5	79
1/4 cup	59 ml	20	59
1 TBS	15 ml	5	15
1 1/2 tsp	7.5 ml	2.5	7.5
1 tsp	5 ml	2	5

1 cup green beans + 3 cups water = 3 cups green beans

Green Peas, Dehydrated

Measurements		Product (ml)	Water (ml)
US	Metric		
1 cup	237 ml	118.5	237
3/4 cup	178 ml	89	178
1/2 cup	118.5 ml	59	118.5
1/3 cup	79 ml	39.5	79
1/4 cup	59 ml	29.5	59
1 TBS	15 ml	7.5	15
1 1/2 tsp	7.5 ml	4	7.5
1 tsp	5 ml	2.5	5

1 cup green peas + 2 cups water = 2 cups green peas

Green Peas, Freeze-Dried

Measurements		Product (ml)	Water (ml)
US	Metric		
1 cup	237 ml	118.5	237
3/4 cup	178 ml	89	178
1/2 cup	118.5 ml	59	118.5
1/3 cup	79 ml	39.5	79
1/4 cup	59 ml	29.5	59
1 TBS	15 ml	7.5	15
1 1/2 tsp	7.5 ml	4	7.5
1 tsp	5 ml	2.5	5

1/2 cup green peas + 1 cup water = 1 cup green peas

Jalapeno Dices, Dehydrated

Measurements		Product (ml)	Water (ml)
US	Metric		
1 cup	237 ml	95	190
3/4 cup	178 ml	71	142.5
1/2 cup	118.5 ml	47.5	95
1/3 cup	79 ml	32	63
1/4 cup	59 ml	24	47
1 TBS	15 ml	6	12
1 1/2 tsp	7.5 ml	3	6
1 tsp	5 ml	2	4

1 cup jalapeno + 2 cups water = 2 1/2 cups jalapeno

Leeks, Dehydrated

Measurements		Product (ml)	Water (ml)
US	Metric		
1 cup	237 ml	190	379
3/4 cup	178 ml	142.5	285
1/2 cup	118.5 ml	95	190
1/3 cup	79 ml	63	126.5
1/4 cup	59 ml	47	94.5
1 TBS	15 ml	12	24
1 1/2 tsp	7.5 ml	6	12
1 tsp	5 ml	4	8

1 cup leeks + 2 cups water = 1 1/4 cups leeks

Mushrooms, Dehydrated

Measurements		Product (ml)	Water (ml)
US	Metric		
1 cup	237 ml	237	474
3/4 cup	178 ml	178	356
1/2 cup	118.5 ml	118.5	237
1/3 cup	79 ml	79	158
1/4 cup	59 ml	59	118
1 TBS	15 ml	15	30
1 1/2 tsp	7.5 ml	7.5	15
1 tsp	5 ml	5	10

1 cup mushrooms + 2 cups water = 1 cup mushrooms

Mushrooms, Freeze-Dried

Measurements		Product (ml)	Water (ml)
US	Metric		
1 cup	237 ml	237	474
3/4 cup	178 ml	178	356
1/2 cup	118.5 ml	118.5	237
1/3 cup	79 ml	79	158
1/4 cup	59 ml	59	118
1 TBS	15 ml	15	30
1 1/2 tsp	7.5 ml	7.5	15
1 tsp	5 ml	5	10

1 cup mushrooms + 2 cups water = 1 cup mushrooms

Mushrooms, Shiitake, Dehydrated

Measurements		Product (ml)	Water (ml)
US	Metric		
1 cup	237 ml	237	474
3/4 cup	178 ml	178	356
1/2 cup	118.5 ml	118.5	237
1/3 cup	79 ml	79	158
1/4 cup	59 ml	59	118
1 TBS	15 ml	15	30
1 1/2 tsp	7.5 ml	7.5	15
1 tsp	5 ml	5	10

1 cup Shiitake mushrooms + 2 cups water = 1 cup Shiitake mushrooms

Okra, Freeze-Dried

Measurements		Product (ml)	Water (ml)
US	Metric		
1 cup	237 ml	237	474
3/4 cup	178 ml	178	356
1/2 cup	118.5 ml	118.5	237
1/3 cup	79 ml	79	158
1/4 cup	59 ml	59	118
1 TBS	15 ml	15	30
1 1/2 tsp	7.5 ml	7.5	15
1 tsp	5 ml	5	10

1 cup okra + 2 cups water = 1 cup okra

Onions, Dehydrated

Measurements		Product (ml)	Water (ml)
US	Metric		
1 cup	237 ml	79	158
3/4 cup	178 ml	59.5	119
1/2 cup	118.5 ml	39.5	79
1/3 cup	79 ml	26.5	53
1/4 cup	59 ml	20	39.5
1 TBS	15 ml	5	10
1 1/2 tsp	7.5 ml	2.5	5
1 tsp	5 ml	2	3.5

1 cup onions + 2 cups water = 3 cups onions

Onions, Freeze-Dried

Measurements		Product (ml)	Water (ml)
US	Metric		
1 cup	237 ml	237	711
3/4 cup	178 ml	178	534
1/2 cup	118.5 ml	118.5	355.5
1/3 cup	79 ml	79	237
1/4 cup	59 ml	59	177
1 TBS	15 ml	15	45
1 1/2 tsp	7.5 ml	7.5	22.5
1 tsp	5 ml	5	15

4 tsp onions + 1/4 cup water = 4 tsp onions

Diced Potatoes, Dehydrated

Measurements		Product (ml)	Water (ml)
US	Metric		
1 cup	237 ml	118.5	237
3/4 cup	178 ml	89	178
1/2 cup	118.5 ml	59	118.5
1/3 cup	79 ml	39.5	79
1/4 cup	59 ml	29.5	59
1 TBS	15 ml	7.5	15
1 1/2 tsp	7.5 ml	4	7.5
1 tsp	5 ml	2.5	5

1 cup diced potatoes + 2 cups water = 2 cups potatoes

Diced Potatoes, Freeze-Dried

Measurements		Product (ml)	Water (ml)
US	Metric		
1 cup	237 ml	237	474
3/4 cup	178 ml	178	356
1/2 cup	118.5 ml	118.5	237
1/3 cup	79 ml	79	158
1/4 cup	59 ml	59	118
1 TBS	15 ml	15	30
1 1/2 tsp	7.5 ml	7.5	15
1 tsp	5 ml	5	10

1 cup diced potatoes + 2 cups water = 1 cup potatoes

Potato Flakes, Dehydrated

Measurements		Product (ml)	Water or Milk (ml)
US	Metric		
1 cup	237 ml	158	211
3/4 cup	178 ml	119	158
1/2 cup	118.5 ml	79	105.5
1/3 cup	79 ml	53	70
1/4 cup	59 ml	39.5	52.5
1 TBS	15 ml	10	13.5
1 1/2 tsp	7.5 ml	5	7
1 tsp	5 ml	3.5	4.5

2 cups potatoes + 2 2/3 cups water (or milk) = 3 cups potatoes

Sliced Potatoes, Dehydrated

Measurements		Product (ml)	Water (ml)
US	Metric		
1 cup	237 ml	118.5	237
3/4 cup	178 ml	89	178
1/2 cup	118.5 ml	59	118.5
1/3 cup	79 ml	39.5	79
1/4 cup	59 ml	29.5	59
1 TBS	15 ml	7.5	15
1 1/2 tsp	7.5 ml	4	7.5
1 tsp	5 ml	2.5	5

1 cup sliced potatoes + 2 cups water = 2 cups potatoes

Hash Brown Potatoes, Dehydrated

Measurements		Product (ml)	Water (ml)
US	Metric		
1 cup	237 ml	79	316
3/4 cup	178 ml	59.5	237.5
1/2 cup	118.5 ml	39.5	158
1/3 cup	79 ml	26.5	105.5
1/4 cup	59 ml	20	79
1 TBS	15 ml	5	20
1 1/2 tsp	7.5 ml	2.5	10
1 tsp	5 ml	2	7

1/2 cup hash brown potatoes + 2 cups water = 1 1/2 cups hash brown potatoes

Pumpkin Powder, Dehydrated

Measurements		Product (ml)	Water (ml)
US	Metric		
1 cup	237 ml	39.5	197.5
3/4 cup	178 ml	30	148.5
1/2 cup	118.5 ml	20	99
1/3 cup	79 ml	13	66
1/4 cup	59 ml	10	49
1 TBS	15 ml	2.5	12.5
1 1/2 tsp	7.5 ml	1	6
1 tsp	5 ml	1	4

1 cup pumpkin powder + 5 cups water = 6 cups pumpkin puree

Shallots, Dehydrated

Measurements		Product (ml)	Water (ml)
US	Metric		
1 cup	237 ml	79	158
3/4 cup	178 ml	59.5	119
1/2 cup	118.5 ml	39.5	79
1/3 cup	79 ml	26.5	53
1/4 cup	59 ml	20	39.5
1 TBS	15 ml	5	10
1 1/2 tsp	7.5 ml	2.5	5
1 tsp	5 ml	2	3.5

1 cup shallots + 2 cups water = 3 cups shallots

Sweet Peas, Dehydrated

Measurements		Product (ml)	Water (ml)
US	Metric		
1 cup	237 ml	118.5	237
3/4 cup	178 ml	89	178
1/2 cup	118.5 ml	59	118.5
1/3 cup	79 ml	39.5	79
1/4 cup	59 ml	29.5	59
1 TBS	15 ml	7.5	15
1 1/2 tsp	7.5 ml	4	7.5
1 tsp	5 ml	2.5	5

1 cup sweet peas + 2 cups water = 2 cups sweet peas

Sweet Potato Powder, Dehydrated

Measurements		Product (ml)	Water (ml)
US	Metric		
1 cup	237 ml	237	237
3/4 cup	178 ml	178	178
1/2 cup	118.5 ml	118.5	118.5
1/3 cup	79 ml	79	79
1/4 cup	59 ml	59	59
1 TBS	15 ml	15	15
1 1/2 tsp	7.5 ml	7.5	7.5
1 tsp	5 ml	5	5

1 cup sweet potato powder + 1 cup water = 1 cup sweet potato puree

Sweet Potatoes, Dehydrated

Measurements		Product (ml)	Water (ml)
US	Metric		
1 cup	237 ml	118.5	237
3/4 cup	178 ml	89	178
1/2 cup	118.5 ml	59	118.5
1/3 cup	79 ml	39.5	79
1/4 cup	59 ml	29.5	59
1 TBS	15 ml	7.5	15
1 1/2 tsp	7.5 ml	4	7.5
1 tsp	5 ml	2.5	5

1 cup sweet potatoes + 2 cups water = 2 cups sweet potatoes

Sweet Potatoes, Freeze-Dried

Measurements		Product (ml)	Water (ml)
US	Metric		
1 cup	237 ml	237	474
3/4 cup	178 ml	178	356
1/2 cup	118.5 ml	118.5	237
1/3 cup	79 ml	79	158
1/4 cup	59 ml	59	118
1 TBS	15 ml	15	30
1 1/2 tsp	7.5 ml	7.5	15
1 tsp	5 ml	5	10

1 cup sweet potatoes + 2 cups water = 1 cup sweet potatoes

Spinach, Dehydrated

Measurements		Product (ml)	Water (ml)
US	Metric		
1 cup	237 ml	158	316
3/4 cup	178 ml	119	237.5
1/2 cup	118.5 ml	79	158
1/3 cup	79 ml	53	105.5
1/4 cup	59 ml	39.5	79
1 TBS	15 ml	10	20
1 1/2 tsp	7.5 ml	5	10
1 tsp	5 ml	3.5	7

1 cup spinach + 2 cups water = 1 1/2 cups spinach

Spinach, Freeze-Dried

Measurements		Product (ml)	Water (ml)
US	Metric		
1 cup	237 ml	237	474
3/4 cup	178 ml	178	356
1/2 cup	118.5 ml	118.5	237
1/3 cup	79 ml	79	158
1/4 cup	59 ml	59	118
1 TBS	15 ml	15	30
1 1/2 tsp	7.5 ml	7.5	15
1 tsp	5 ml	5	10

1 cup spinach + 2 cups water = 1 cup spinach

Tomato Dices, Dehydrated

Measurements		Product (ml)	Water (ml)
US	Metric		
1 cup	237 ml	47.5	190
3/4 cup	178 ml	35.5	142.5
1/2 cup	118.5 ml	24	95
1/3 cup	79 ml	16	63
1/4 cup	59 ml	12	47
1 TBS	15 ml	3	12
1 1/2 tsp	7.5 ml	1.5	6
1 tsp	5 ml	1	4

1 cup tomato dices + 4 cups water = 5 cups tomatoes

Tomato Dices, Freeze-Dried

Measurements		Product (ml)	Water (ml)
US	Metric		
1 cup	237 ml	237	395
3/4 cup	178 ml	178	297
1/2 cup	118.5 ml	118.5	197.5
1/3 cup	79 ml	79	132
1/4 cup	59 ml	59	98.5
1 TBS	15 ml	15	25
1 1/2 tsp	7.5 ml	7.5	12.5
1 tsp	5 ml	5	8.5

2/3 cup tomato dices + 1 cup water = 2/3 cup tomatoes

Tomato Powder – Paste, Dehydrated

Measurements		Product (ml)	Water (ml)
US	Metric		
1 cup	237 ml	95	190
3/4 cup	178 ml	71	142.5
1/2 cup	118.5 ml	47.5	95
1/3 cup	79 ml	32	63
1/4 cup	59 ml	24	47
1 TBS	15 ml	6	12
1 1/2 tsp	7.5 ml	3	6
1 tsp	5 ml	2	4

1 cup tomato powder + 2 cups water = 2 1/2 cups tomato paste

Tomato Powder – Sauce, Dehydrated

Measurements		Product (ml)	Water (ml)
US	Metric		
1 cup	237 ml	47.5	190
3/4 cup	178 ml	35.5	142.5
1/2 cup	118.5 ml	24	95
1/3 cup	79 ml	16	63
1/4 cup	59 ml	12	47
1 TBS	15 ml	3	12
1 1/2 tsp	7.5 ml	1.5	6
1 tsp	5 ml	1	4

1 cup tomato powder + 4 cups water = 5 cups tomato sauce

Vegetable Soup Mix, Dehydrated

Measurements		Product (ml)	Water (ml)
US	Metric		
1 cup	237 ml	59	237
3/4 cup	178 ml	44.5	178
1/2 cup	118.5 ml	30	118.5
1/3 cup	79 ml	20	79
1/4 cup	59 ml	15	59
1 TBS	15 ml	4	15
1 1/2 tsp	7.5 ml	2	7.5
1 tsp	5 ml	1	5

1/2 cup vegetable soup mix + 2 cups water = 2 cups vegetable soup

Zucchini, Dehydrated

Measurements		Product (ml)	Water (ml)
US	Metric		
1 cup	237 ml	95	190
3/4 cup	178 ml	71	142.5
1/2 cup	118.5 ml	47.5	95
1/3 cup	79 ml	32	63
1/4 cup	59 ml	24	47
1 TBS	15 ml	6	12
1 1/2 tsp	7.5 ml	3	6
1 tsp	5 ml	2	4

1 cup zucchini + 2 cups water = 2 1/2 cups zucchini

Zucchini, Freeze-Dried

Measurements		Product (ml)	Water (ml)
US	Metric		
1 cup	237 ml	237	474
3/4 cup	178 ml	178	356
1/2 cup	118.5 ml	118.5	237
1/3 cup	79 ml	79	158
1/4 cup	59 ml	59	118
1 TBS	15 ml	15	30
1 1/2 tsp	7.5 ml	7.5	15
1 tsp	5 ml	5	10

1 cup zucchini + 2 cups water = 1 cup zucchini

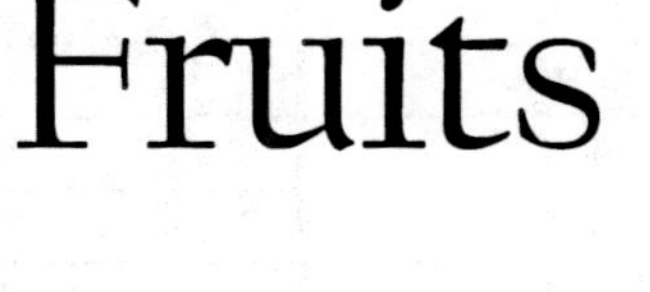

Fruits

Apple Dices, Freeze-Dried

Measurements		Product (ml)	Water (ml)
US	Metric		
1 cup	237 ml	237	237
3/4 cup	178 ml	178	178
1/2 cup	118.5 ml	118.5	118.5
1/3 cup	79 ml	79	79
1/4 cup	59 ml	59	59
1 TBS	15 ml	15	15
1 1/2 tsp	7.5 ml	7.5	7.5
1 tsp	5 ml	5	5

1 cup apple dices + 1 cup water = 1 cup apple dices

Apricot, Freeze-Dried

Measurements		Product (ml)	Water (ml)
US	Metric		
1 cup	237 ml	237	237
3/4 cup	178 ml	178	178
1/2 cup	118.5 ml	118.5	118.5
1/3 cup	79 ml	79	79
1/4 cup	59 ml	59	59
1 TBS	15 ml	15	15
1 1/2 tsp	7.5 ml	7.5	7.5
1 tsp	5 ml	5	5

1 cup apricot + 1 cup water = 1 cup apricot

Banana Slices, Freeze-Dried

Measurements		Product (ml)	Water (ml)
US	Metric		
1 cup	237 ml	237	237
3/4 cup	178 ml	178	178
1/2 cup	118.5 ml	118.5	118.5
1/3 cup	79 ml	79	79
1/4 cup	59 ml	59	59
1 TBS	15 ml	15	15
1 1/2 tsp	7.5 ml	7.5	7.5
1 tsp	5 ml	5	5

1 cup banana slices + 1 cup water = 1 cup banana slices

Cherries, Freeze-Dried

Measurements		Product (ml)	Water (ml)
US	Metric		
1 cup	237 ml	237	237
3/4 cup	178 ml	178	178
1/2 cup	118.5 ml	118.5	118.5
1/3 cup	79 ml	79	79
1/4 cup	59 ml	59	59
1 TBS	15 ml	15	15
1 1/2 tsp	7.5 ml	7.5	7.5
1 tsp	5 ml	5	5

1 cup cherries + 1 cup water = 1 cup cherries

Mango, Freeze-Dried

Measurements		Product (ml)	Water (ml)
US	Metric		
1 cup	237 ml	237	237
3/4 cup	178 ml	178	178
1/2 cup	118.5 ml	118.5	118.5
1/3 cup	79 ml	79	79
1/4 cup	59 ml	59	59
1 TBS	15 ml	15	15
1 1/2 tsp	7.5 ml	7.5	7.5
1 tsp	5 ml	5	5

1 cup mango + 1 cup water = 1 cup mango

Papaya, Freeze-Dried

Measurements		Product (ml)	Water (ml)
US	Metric		
1 cup	237 ml	237	237
3/4 cup	178 ml	178	178
1/2 cup	118.5 ml	118.5	118.5
1/3 cup	79 ml	79	79
1/4 cup	59 ml	59	59
1 TBS	15 ml	15	15
1 1/2 tsp	7.5 ml	7.5	7.5
1 tsp	5 ml	5	5

1 cup papaya + 1 cup water = 1 cup papaya

Pineapple, Freeze-Dried

Measurements		Product (ml)	Water (ml)
US	Metric		
1 cup	237 ml	237	237
3/4 cup	178 ml	178	178
1/2 cup	118.5 ml	118.5	118.5
1/3 cup	79 ml	79	79
1/4 cup	59 ml	59	59
1 TBS	15 ml	15	15
1 1/2 tsp	7.5 ml	7.5	7.5
1 tsp	5 ml	5	5

1 cup pineapple + 1 cup water = 1 cup pineapple

Strawberries, Freeze-Dried

Measurements		Product (ml)	Water (ml)
US	Metric		
1 cup	237 ml	237	237
3/4 cup	178 ml	178	178
1/2 cup	118.5 ml	118.5	118.5
1/3 cup	79 ml	79	79
1/4 cup	59 ml	59	59
1 TBS	15 ml	15	15
1 1/2 tsp	7.5 ml	7.5	7.5
1 tsp	5 ml	5	5

1 cup strawberries + 1 cup water = 1 cup strawberries

Blueberries, Freeze-Dried

Measurements		Product (ml)	Water (ml)
US	Metric		
1 cup	237 ml	237	237
3/4 cup	178 ml	178	178
1/2 cup	118.5 ml	118.5	118.5
1/3 cup	79 ml	79	79
1/4 cup	59 ml	59	59
1 TBS	15 ml	15	15
1 1/2 tsp	7.5 ml	7.5	7.5
1 tsp	5 ml	5	5

1 cup blueberries + 1 cup water = 1 cup blueberries

Raspberries, Freeze-Dried

Measurements		Product (ml)	Water (ml)
US	Metric		
1 cup	237 ml	237	237
3/4 cup	178 ml	178	178
1/2 cup	118.5 ml	118.5	118.5
1/3 cup	79 ml	79	79
1/4 cup	59 ml	59	59
1 TBS	15 ml	15	15
1 1/2 tsp	7.5 ml	7.5	7.5
1 tsp	5 ml	5	5

1 cup raspberries + 1 cup water = 1 cup raspberries

Blackberries, Freeze-Dried

Measurements		Product (ml)	Water (ml)
US	Metric		
1 cup	237 ml	237	237
3/4 cup	178 ml	178	178
1/2 cup	118.5 ml	118.5	118.5
1/3 cup	79 ml	79	79
1/4 cup	59 ml	59	59
1 TBS	15 ml	15	15
1 1/2 tsp	7.5 ml	7.5	7.5
1 tsp	5 ml	5	5

1 cup blackberries + 1 cup water = 1 cup blackberries

Mixed Berries, Freeze-Dried

Measurements		Product (ml)	Water (ml)
US	Metric		
1 cup	237 ml	237	237
3/4 cup	178 ml	178	178
1/2 cup	118.5 ml	118.5	118.5
1/3 cup	79 ml	79	79
1/4 cup	59 ml	59	59
1 TBS	15 ml	15	15
1 1/2 tsp	7.5 ml	7.5	7.5
1 tsp	5 ml	5	5

1 cup mixed berries + 1 cup water = 1 cup mixed berries

Orange Slices, Freeze-Dried

Measurements		Product (ml)	Water (ml)
US	Metric		
1 cup	237 ml	237	237
3/4 cup	178 ml	178	178
1/2 cup	118.5 ml	118.5	118.5
1/3 cup	79 ml	79	79
1/4 cup	59 ml	59	59
1 TBS	15 ml	15	15
1 1/2 tsp	7.5 ml	7.5	7.5
1 tsp	5 ml	5	5

1 cup orange slices + 1 cup water = 1 cup orange slices

Pears, Freeze-Dried

Measurements		Product (ml)	Water (ml)
US	Metric		
1 cup	237 ml	237	237
3/4 cup	178 ml	178	178
1/2 cup	118.5 ml	118.5	118.5
1/3 cup	79 ml	79	79
1/4 cup	59 ml	59	59
1 TBS	15 ml	15	15
1 1/2 tsp	7.5 ml	7.5	7.5
1 tsp	5 ml	5	5

1 cup pears + 1 cup water = 1 cup pears

Peaches, Freeze-Dried

Measurements		Product (ml)	Water (ml)
US	Metric		
1 cup	237 ml	237	237
3/4 cup	178 ml	178	178
1/2 cup	118.5 ml	118.5	118.5
1/3 cup	79 ml	79	79
1/4 cup	59 ml	59	59
1 TBS	15 ml	15	15
1 1/2 tsp	7.5 ml	7.5	7.5
1 tsp	5 ml	5	5

1 cup peaches + 1 cup water = 1 cup peaches

Raisins, Freeze-Dried

Measurements		Product (ml)	Water (ml)
US	Metric		
1 cup	237 ml	237	237
3/4 cup	178 ml	178	178
1/2 cup	118.5 ml	118.5	118.5
1/3 cup	79 ml	79	79
1/4 cup	59 ml	59	59
1 TBS	15 ml	15	15
1 1/2 tsp	7.5 ml	7.5	7.5
1 tsp	5 ml	5	5

1 cup raisins + 1 cup water = 1 cup raisins

Dehydrated Beans & Legumes

Black Beans, Dehydrated

Measurements		Product (ml)	Water (ml)
US	Metric		
1 cup	237 ml	118.5	118.5
3/4 cup	178 ml	89	89
1/2 cup	118.5 ml	59	59
1/3 cup	79 ml	39.5	39.5
1/4 cup	59 ml	29.5	29.5
1 TBS	15 ml	7.5	7.5
1 1/2 tsp	7.5 ml	4	4
1 tsp	5 ml	2.5	2.5

1 cup black beans + 1 cup water = 2 cups black beans

Dark Kidney Beans, Dehydrated

Measurements		Product (ml)	Water (ml)
US	Metric		
1 cup	237 ml	118.5	118.5
3/4 cup	178 ml	89	89
1/2 cup	118.5 ml	59	59
1/3 cup	79 ml	39.5	39.5
1/4 cup	59 ml	29.5	29.5
1 TBS	15 ml	7.5	7.5
1 1/2 tsp	7.5 ml	4	4
1 tsp	5 ml	2.5	2.5

1 cup dark kidney beans + 1 cup water = 2 cups dark kidney beans

Garbanzo Beans, Dehydrated

Measurements		Product (ml)	Water (ml)
US	Metric		
1 cup	237 ml	118.5	118.5
3/4 cup	178 ml	89	89
1/2 cup	118.5 ml	59	59
1/3 cup	79 ml	39.5	39.5
1/4 cup	59 ml	29.5	29.5
1 TBS	15 ml	7.5	7.5
1 1/2 tsp	7.5 ml	4	4
1 tsp	5 ml	2.5	2.5

1 cup garbanzo beans + 1 cup water = 2 cups garbanzo beans

Great Northern Beans, Dehydrated

Measurements		Product (ml)	Water (ml)
US	Metric		
1 cup	237 ml	118.5	118.5
3/4 cup	178 ml	89	89
1/2 cup	118.5 ml	59	59
1/3 cup	79 ml	39.5	39.5
1/4 cup	59 ml	29.5	29.5
1 TBS	15 ml	7.5	7.5
1 1/2 tsp	7.5 ml	4	4
1 tsp	5 ml	2.5	2.5

1 cup great northern beans + 1 cup water = 2 cups great northern beans

Lentils, Dehydrated

Measurements		Product (ml)	Water (ml)
US	Metric		
1 cup	237 ml	118.5	118.5
3/4 cup	178 ml	89	89
1/2 cup	118.5 ml	59	59
1/3 cup	79 ml	39.5	39.5
1/4 cup	59 ml	29.5	29.5
1 TBS	15 ml	7.5	7.5
1 1/2 tsp	7.5 ml	4	4
1 tsp	5 ml	2.5	2.5

1 cup lentils + 1 cup water = 2 cups lentils

Navy Beans, Dehydrated

Measurements		Product (ml)	Water (ml)
US	Metric		
1 cup	237 ml	118.5	118.5
3/4 cup	178 ml	89	89
1/2 cup	118.5 ml	59	59
1/3 cup	79 ml	39.5	39.5
1/4 cup	59 ml	29.5	29.5
1 TBS	15 ml	7.5	7.5
1 1/2 tsp	7.5 ml	4	4
1 tsp	5 ml	2.5	2.5

1 cup navy beans + 1 cup water = 2 cups navy beans

Pinto Beans, Dehydrated

Measurements		Product (ml)	Water (ml)
US	Metric		
1 cup	237 ml	118.5	118.5
3/4 cup	178 ml	89	89
1/2 cup	118.5 ml	59	59
1/3 cup	79 ml	39.5	39.5
1/4 cup	59 ml	29.5	29.5
1 TBS	15 ml	7.5	7.5
1 1/2 tsp	7.5 ml	4	4
1 tsp	5 ml	2.5	2.5

1 cup pinto beans + 1 cup water = 2 cups pinto beans

Red Beans, Dehydrated

Measurements		Product (ml)	Water (ml)
US	Metric		
1 cup	237 ml	118.5	118.5
3/4 cup	178 ml	89	89
1/2 cup	118.5 ml	59	59
1/3 cup	79 ml	39.5	39.5
1/4 cup	59 ml	29.5	29.5
1 TBS	15 ml	7.5	7.5
1 1/2 tsp	7.5 ml	4	4
1 tsp	5 ml	2.5	2.5

1 cup red beans + 1 cup water = 2 cups red beans

Split Peas, Dehydrated

Measurements		Product (ml)	Water (ml)
US	Metric		
1 cup	237 ml	118.5	118.5
3/4 cup	178 ml	89	89
1/2 cup	118.5 ml	59	59
1/3 cup	79 ml	39.5	39.5
1/4 cup	59 ml	29.5	29.5
1 TBS	15 ml	7.5	7.5
1 1/2 tsp	7.5 ml	4	4
1 tsp	5 ml	2.5	2.5

1 cup split peas + 1 cup water = 2 cups split peas

Dried Beans & Legumes

Beans, Dried

Dried beans are a great source of protein, and like their dehydrated and freeze-dried counterparts, they have a long shelf life. As a general rule, one cup of dried beans will produce three cups of cooked beans.

There are MANY varieties of dried beans including: Adzuki Beans, Anasazi Beans, Appaloosa Beans, Black Beans, Blackeyed Peas, Calypso Beans, Cannellini Beans, Christmas Lima Beans, Cranberry Beans, Dapple Grey Beans, European Soldier Beans, Fava Beans, Flageolet Beans, Garbanzo Beans, Great Northern Beans, Green Split Peas, Habas Beans, Jackson Wonder Beans, Jacobs Cattle Beans, Kidney Beans, Lentils, Lima Beans, Lupini Beans, Marrow Beans, Mayocoba Beans, Moccasin Beans, Mung Beans, Navy Beans, Orca Beans, Peruanao Beans, Pigeon Peas, Pink Beans, Pinto Beans, Provence Beans, Rattlesnake Beans, Rice Beans, Red Beans, Snow Cap Beans, White Emergo Beans, and Yellow Eye Beans.

Unlike dehydrated beans, dried beans need to be pre-soaked prior to cooking. When pre-soaking the beans, cover the beans with two inches of water, and soak for a minimum of two hours. Pour off the soaking water, add fresh water, and cook according to the recipe. The chart below shows the amount of dried beans needed to produce the desired amount of cooked beans.

Cooked Amount		Dried Beans US	Dried Beans Metric (ml)
US	Metric (ml)		
1 cup	237	1/3 cup	79
3/4 cup	178	1/4 cup	59
1/2 cup	118.5	2 TBS + 2 tsp	39.5
1/3 cup	79	1 TBS + 2 tsp	25
1/4 cup	59	1 TBS + 1 tsp	20
1 TBS	15	1 tsp	5
1 1/2 tsp	7.5	1/2 tsp	2.5
1 tsp	5	1/3 tsp	2

1 cup dried beans = 3 cups cooked beans

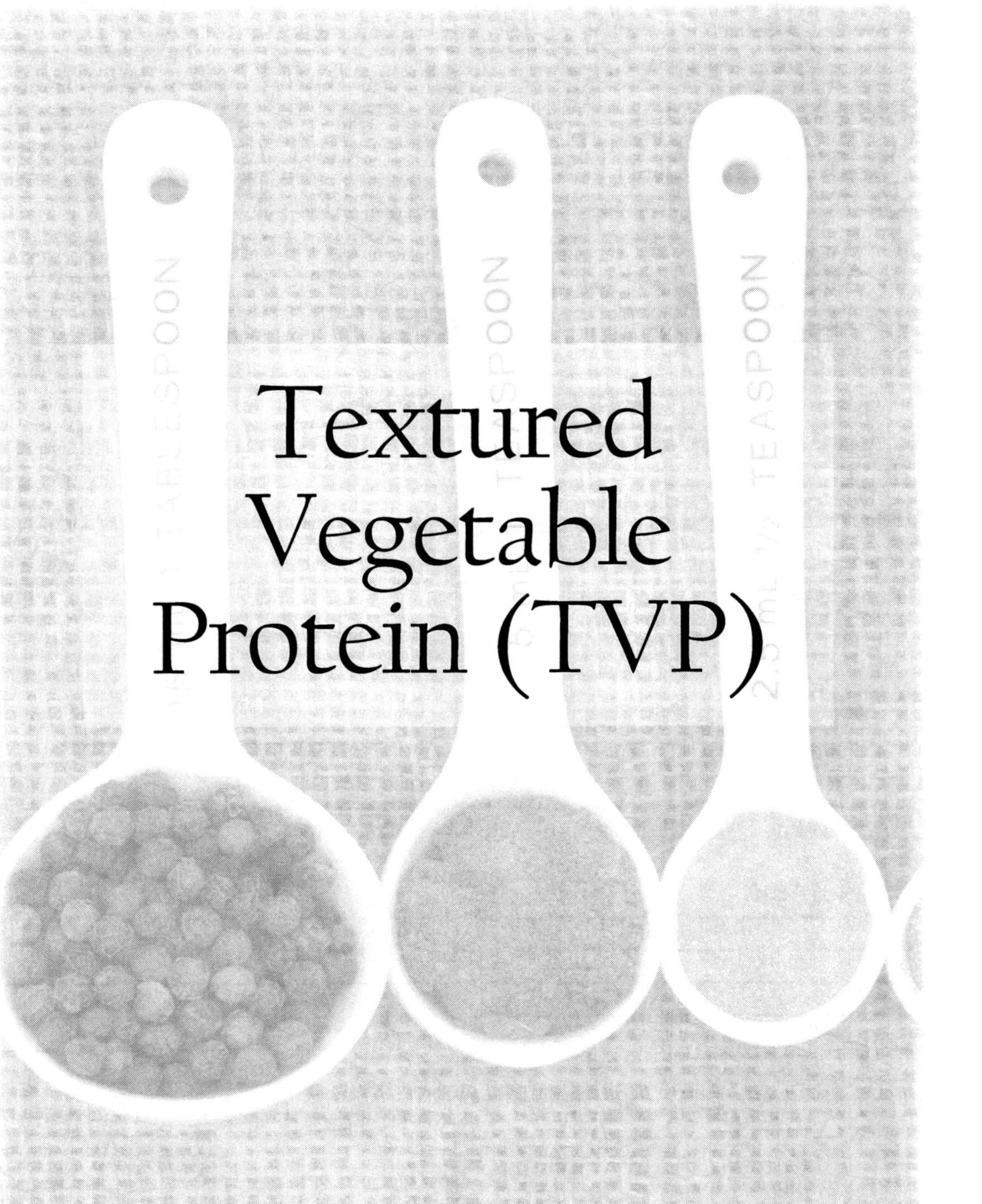

Textured Vegetable Protein (TVP)

Bacon Bits, TVP

Measurements		Product (ml)	Water (ml)
US	Metric		
1 cup	237 ml	237	237
3/4 cup	178 ml	178	178
1/2 cup	118.5 ml	118.5	118.5
1/3 cup	79 ml	79	79
1/4 cup	59 ml	59	59
1 TBS	15 ml	15	15
1 1/2 tsp	7.5 ml	7.5	7.5
1 tsp	5 ml	5	5

1 cup bacon bits TVP + 1 cup water = 1 cup bacon bits

Beef Bits, TVP

Measurements		Product (ml)	Water (ml)
US	Metric		
1 cup	237 ml	79	158
3/4 cup	178 ml	59.5	119
1/2 cup	118.5 ml	39.5	79
1/3 cup	79 ml	26.5	53
1/4 cup	59 ml	20	39.5
1 TBS	15 ml	5	10
1 1/2 tsp	7.5 ml	2.5	5
1 tsp	5 ml	2	3.5

1 cup beef bits TVP + 2 cups water = 3 cups beef bits

Beef Chunks, TVP

Measurements		Product (ml)	Water (ml)
US	Metric		
1 cup	237 ml	158	316
3/4 cup	178 ml	119	237.5
1/2 cup	118.5 ml	79	158
1/3 cup	79 ml	53	105.5
1/4 cup	59 ml	39.5	79
1 TBS	15 ml	10	20
1 1/2 tsp	7.5 ml	5	10
1 tsp	5 ml	3.5	7

1 cup beef chunks TVP + 2 cups water = 1 1/2 cups beef chunks

Chicken Bits, TVP

Measurements		Product (ml)	Water (ml)
US	Metric		
1 cup	237 ml	95	190
3/4 cup	178 ml	71	142.5
1/2 cup	118.5 ml	47.5	95
1/3 cup	79 ml	32	63
1/4 cup	59 ml	24	47
1 TBS	15 ml	6	12
1 1/2 tsp	7.5 ml	3	6
1 tsp	5 ml	2	4

1 cup chicken bits TVP + 2 cups water = 2 1/2 cups chicken bits

Chicken Chunks, TVP

Measurements		Product (ml)	Water (ml)
US	Metric		
1 cup	237 ml	158	316
3/4 cup	178 ml	119	237.5
1/2 cup	118.5 ml	79	158
1/3 cup	79 ml	53	105.5
1/4 cup	59 ml	39.5	79
1 TBS	15 ml	10	20
1 1/2 tsp	7.5 ml	5	10
1 tsp	5 ml	3.5	7

1 cup TVP chicken chunks + 2 cups water = 1 1/2 cups chicken chunks

Ham Bits, TVP

Measurements		Product (ml)	Water (ml)
US	Metric		
1 cup	237 ml	118.5	237
3/4 cup	178 ml	89	178
1/2 cup	118.5 ml	59	118.5
1/3 cup	79 ml	39.5	79
1/4 cup	59 ml	29.5	59
1 TBS	15 ml	7.5	15
1 1/2 tsp	7.5 ml	4	7.5
1 tsp	5 ml	2.5	5

1 cup ham bits TVP + 2 cups water = 2 cups ham bits

Pepperoni, TVP

Measurements		Product (ml)	Water (ml)
US	Metric		
1 cup	237 ml	237	237
3/4 cup	178 ml	178	178
1/2 cup	118.5 ml	118.5	118.5
1/3 cup	79 ml	79	79
1/4 cup	59 ml	59	59
1 TBS	15 ml	15	15
1 1/2 tsp	7.5 ml	7.5	7.5
1 tsp	5 ml	5	5

1 cup pepperoni TVP + 1 cup water = 1 cup pepperoni

Plain, TVP

Measurements		Product (ml)	Water (ml)
US	Metric		
1 cup	237 ml	105.5	211
3/4 cup	178 ml	79	158
1/2 cup	118.5 ml	53	105.5
1/3 cup	79 ml	35	70
1/4 cup	59 ml	26	52.5
1 TBS	15 ml	7	13.5
1 1/2 tsp	7.5 ml	3.5	7
1 tsp	5 ml	2	4.5

1 cup plain TVP + 2 cups water = 2 1/4 cups TVP

Sausage Bits, TVP

Measurements		Product (ml)	Water (ml)
US	Metric		
1 cup	237 ml	158	158
3/4 cup	178 ml	119	119
1/2 cup	118.5 ml	79	79
1/3 cup	79 ml	53	53
1/4 cup	59 ml	39.5	39.5
1 TBS	15 ml	10	10
1 1/2 tsp	7.5 ml	5	5
1 tsp	5 ml	3.5	3.5

2/3 cup sausage bits TVP + 2/3 cup water = 1 cup sausage bits

Sloppy Joe Mix, TVP

Measurements		Product (ml)	Water (ml)
US	Metric		
1 cup	237 ml	118.5	237
3/4 cup	178 ml	89	178
1/2 cup	118.5 ml	59	118.5
1/3 cup	79 ml	39.5	79
1/4 cup	59 ml	29.5	59
1 TBS	15 ml	7.5	15
1 1/2 tsp	7.5 ml	4	7.5
1 tsp	5 ml	2.5	5

1 cup Sloppy Joe mix TVP + 2 cups water = 2 cups Sloppy Joe

Taco Bits, TVP

Measurements		Product (ml)	Water (ml)
US	Metric		
1 cup	237 ml	118.5	237
3/4 cup	178 ml	89	178
1/2 cup	118.5 ml	59	118.5
1/3 cup	79 ml	39.5	79
1/4 cup	59 ml	29.5	59
1 TBS	15 ml	7.5	15
1 1/2 tsp	7.5 ml	4	7.5
1 tsp	5 ml	2.5	5

1 cup taco bits + 2 cups water = 2 cups taco bits

Freeze-Dried Meat

Beef – Ground, Freeze-Dried

Measurements		Product (ml)	Water (ml)
US	Metric		
1 cup	237 ml	237	474
3/4 cup	178 ml	178	356
1/2 cup	118.5 ml	118.5	237
1/3 cup	79 ml	79	158
1/4 cup	59 ml	59	118
1 TBS	15 ml	15	30
1 1/2 tsp	7.5 ml	7.5	15
1 tsp	5 ml	5	10

1 cup ground beef + 2 cups water = 1 cup ground beef (drain excess water)

Beef – Roast, Freeze-Dried

Measurements		Product (ml)	Water (ml)
US	Metric		
1 cup	237 ml	237	474
3/4 cup	178 ml	178	356
1/2 cup	118.5 ml	118.5	237
1/3 cup	79 ml	79	158
1/4 cup	59 ml	59	118
1 TBS	15 ml	15	30
1 1/2 tsp	7.5 ml	7.5	15
1 tsp	5 ml	5	10

1 cup roast beef + 2 cups water = 1 cup roast beef (drain excess water)

Chicken Dices, Freeze-Dried

Measurements		Product (ml)	Water (ml)
US	Metric		
1 cup	237 ml	237	474
3/4 cup	178 ml	178	356
1/2 cup	118.5 ml	118.5	237
1/3 cup	79 ml	79	158
1/4 cup	59 ml	59	118
1 TBS	15 ml	15	30
1 1/2 tsp	7.5 ml	7.5	15
1 tsp	5 ml	5	10

1 cup chicken dices + 2 cups water = 1 cup chicken dices (drain excess water)

Chicken Slices, Freeze-Dried

Measurements		Product (ml)	Water (ml)
US	Metric		
1 cup	237 ml	237	474
3/4 cup	178 ml	178	356
1/2 cup	118.5 ml	118.5	237
1/3 cup	79 ml	79	158
1/4 cup	59 ml	59	118
1 TBS	15 ml	15	30
1 1/2 tsp	7.5 ml	7.5	15
1 tsp	5 ml	5	10

1 cup chicken + 2 cups water = 1 cup chicken slices (drain excess water)

Ham Dices, Freeze-Dried

Measurements		Product (ml)	Water (ml)
US	Metric		
1 cup	237 ml	237	474
3/4 cup	178 ml	178	356
1/2 cup	118.5 ml	118.5	237
1/3 cup	79 ml	79	158
1/4 cup	59 ml	59	118
1 TBS	15 ml	15	30
1 1/2 tsp	7.5 ml	7.5	15
1 tsp	5 ml	5	10

1 cup ham dices + 2 cups water = 1 cup ham dices (drain excess water)

Meatballs, Freeze-Dried

Measurements		Product (ml)	Water (ml)
US	Metric		
1 cup	237 ml	237	474
3/4 cup	178 ml	178	356
1/2 cup	118.5 ml	118.5	237
1/3 cup	79 ml	79	158
1/4 cup	59 ml	59	118
1 TBS	15 ml	15	30
1 1/2 tsp	7.5 ml	7.5	15
1 tsp	5 ml	5	10

1 cup meatballs + 2 cups water = 1 cup meatballs (drain excess water)

Sausage Bits, Freeze-Dried

Measurements		Product (ml)	Water (ml)
US	Metric		
1 cup	237 ml	237	474
3/4 cup	178 ml	178	356
1/2 cup	118.5 ml	118.5	237
1/3 cup	79 ml	79	158
1/4 cup	59 ml	59	118
1 TBS	15 ml	15	30
1 1/2 tsp	7.5 ml	7.5	15
1 tsp	5 ml	5	10

1 cup sausage bits + 2 cups water = 1 cup sausage bits (drain excess water)

Turkey, Freeze-Dried

Measurements		Product (ml)	Water (ml)
US	Metric		
1 cup	237 ml	237	474
3/4 cup	178 ml	178	356
1/2 cup	118.5 ml	118.5	237
1/3 cup	79 ml	79	158
1/4 cup	59 ml	59	118
1 TBS	15 ml	15	30
1 1/2 tsp	7.5 ml	7.5	15
1 tsp	5 ml	5	10

1 cup turkey + 2 cups water = 1 cup turkey (drain excess water)

Cheeses

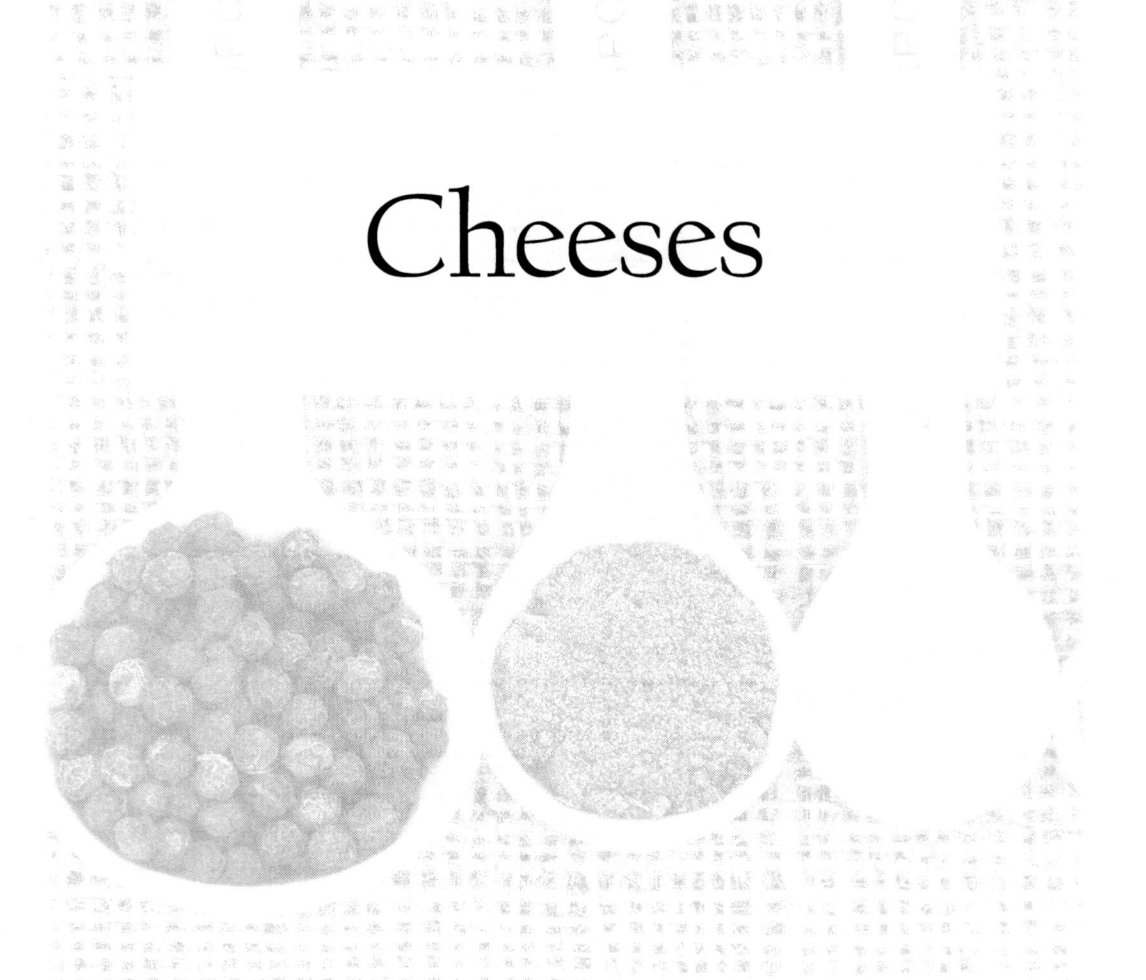

Blue Cheese Powder, Cheese Sauce

Measurements		Product (ml)	Water (ml)
US	Metric		
1 cup	237 ml	59	237
3/4 cup	178 ml	44.5	178
1/2 cup	118.5 ml	30	118.5
1/3 cup	79 ml	20	79
1/4 cup	59 ml	15	59
1 TBS	15 ml	4	15
1 1/2 tsp	7.5 ml	2	7.5
1 tsp	5 ml	1	5

1/2 cup cheese powder + 2 cups water = 2 cups product

Cheddar Powder, Cheese Sauce

Measurements		Product (ml)	Water (ml)
US	Metric		
1 cup	237 ml	59	237
3/4 cup	178 ml	44.5	178
1/2 cup	118.5 ml	30	118.5
1/3 cup	79 ml	20	79
1/4 cup	59 ml	15	59
1 TBS	15 ml	4	15
1 1/2 tsp	7.5 ml	2	7.5
1 tsp	5 ml	1	5

1/2 cup cheese powder + 2 cups water = 2 cups product

Parmesan Cheese Powder, Cheese Sauce

Measurements		Product (ml)	Water (ml)
US	Metric		
1 cup	237 ml	59	237
3/4 cup	178 ml	44.5	178
1/2 cup	118.5 ml	30	118.5
1/3 cup	79 ml	20	79
1/4 cup	59 ml	15	59
1 TBS	15 ml	4	15
1 1/2 tsp	7.5 ml	2	7.5
1 tsp	5 ml	1	5

1/2 cup cheese powder + 2 cups water = 2 cups product

White Cheddar Powder, Cheese Sauce

Measurements		Product (ml)	Water (ml)
US	Metric		
1 cup	237 ml	59	237
3/4 cup	178 ml	44.5	178
1/2 cup	118.5 ml	30	118.5
1/3 cup	79 ml	20	79
1/4 cup	59 ml	15	59
1 TBS	15 ml	4	15
1 1/2 tsp	7.5 ml	2	7.5
1 tsp	5 ml	1	5

1/2 cup cheese powder + 2 cups water = 2 cups product

Cheddar, Freeze-Dried

Measurements		Product (ml)	Water (ml)
US	Metric		
1 cup	237 ml	237	474
3/4 cup	178 ml	178	356
1/2 cup	118.5 ml	118.5	237
1/3 cup	79 ml	79	158
1/4 cup	59 ml	59	118
1 TBS	15 ml	15	30
1 1/2 tsp	7.5 ml	7.5	15
1 tsp	5 ml	5	10

1 cup cheese + 2 cups water = 1 cup product (drain excess water)

Colby, Freeze-Dried

Measurements		Product (ml)	Water (ml)
US	Metric		
1 cup	237 ml	237	237
3/4 cup	178 ml	178	178
1/2 cup	118.5 ml	118.5	118.5
1/3 cup	79 ml	79	79
1/4 cup	59 ml	59	59
1 TBS	15 ml	15	15
1 1/2 tsp	7.5 ml	7.5	7.5
1 tsp	5 ml	5	5

1 cup cheese + 1 cup water = 1 cup product (drain excess water)

Cottage Cheese, Freeze-Dried

Measurements		Product (ml)	Water (ml)
US	Metric		
1 cup	237 ml	237	158
3/4 cup	178 ml	178	119
1/2 cup	118.5 ml	118.5	79
1/3 cup	79 ml	79	53
1/4 cup	59 ml	59	39.5
1 TBS	15 ml	15	10
1 1/2 tsp	7.5 ml	7.5	5
1 tsp	5 ml	5	3.5

1/2 cup dry cottage cheese + 1/3 cup water = 1/2 cup product

Monterey Jack, Freeze-Dried

Measurements		Product (ml)	Water (ml)
US	Metric		
1 cup	237 ml	237	237
3/4 cup	178 ml	178	178
1/2 cup	118.5 ml	118.5	118.5
1/3 cup	79 ml	79	79
1/4 cup	59 ml	59	59
1 TBS	15 ml	15	15
1 1/2 tsp	7.5 ml	7.5	7.5
1 tsp	5 ml	5	5

1 cup cheese + 1 cup water = 1 cup product (drain excess water)

Mozzarella, Freeze-Dried

Measurements		Product (ml)	Water (ml)
US	Metric		
1 cup	237 ml	237	237
3/4 cup	178 ml	178	178
1/2 cup	118.5 ml	118.5	118.5
1/3 cup	79 ml	79	79
1/4 cup	59 ml	59	59
1 TBS	15 ml	15	15
1 1/2 tsp	7.5 ml	7.5	7.5
1 tsp	5 ml	5	5

1 cup cheese + 1 cup water = 1 cup product (drain excess water)

Eggs & Dairy

Whole Eggs, Powdered

Amount	Product (ml)	Water (ml)
12 eggs	360	540
11 eggs	330	495
10 eggs	300	450
9 eggs	270	405
8 eggs	240	360
7 eggs	210	315
6 eggs	180	270
5 eggs	150	225
4 eggs	120	180
3 eggs	90	135
2 eggs	60	90
1 egg	30	45

1 egg = 2 TBS whole egg powder with 3 TBS of water

Egg Whites, Powdered

Amount	Product (ml)	Water (ml)
12 eggs	360	360
11 eggs	330	330
10 eggs	300	300
9 eggs	270	270
8 eggs	240	240
7 eggs	210	210
6 eggs	180	180
5 eggs	150	150
4 eggs	120	120
3 eggs	90	90
2 eggs	60	60
1 egg	30	30

1 egg = 2 TBS egg powder with 2 TBS of water

Sour Cream, Powdered

Measurements		Product (ml)	Water (ml)
US	Metric		
1 cup	237 ml	59	237
3/4 cup	178 ml	44.5	178
1/2 cup	118.5 ml	30	118.5
1/3 cup	79 ml	20	79
1/4 cup	59 ml	15	59
1 TBS	15 ml	4	15
1 1/2 tsp	7.5 ml	2	7.5
1 tsp	5 ml	1	5

1/4 cup sour cream powder + 1 cup water = 1 cup sour cream

Buttermilk, Powdered

Measurements		Product (ml)	Water (ml)
US	Metric		
1 cup	237 ml	79	237
3/4 cup	178 ml	59.5	178
1/2 cup	118.5 ml	39.5	118.5
1/3 cup	79 ml	26.5	79
1/4 cup	59 ml	20	59
1 TBS	15 ml	5	15
1 1/2 tsp	7.5 ml	2.5	7.5
1 tsp	5 ml	2	5

1/3 cup buttermilk powder + 1 cup water = 1 cup buttermilk

Milk, Powdered

Measurements		Product (ml)	Water (ml)
US	Metric		
1 cup	237 ml	59	237
3/4 cup	178 ml	44.5	178
1/2 cup	118.5 ml	30	118.5
1/3 cup	79 ml	20	79
1/4 cup	59 ml	15	59
1 TBS	15 ml	4	15
1 1/2 tsp	7.5 ml	2	7.5
1 tsp	5 ml	1	5

1/4 cup milk powder + 1 cup water = 1 cup milk

Heavy Cream, Powdered

Measurements		Product (ml)	Water (ml)
US	Metric		
1 cup	237 ml	79	237
3/4 cup	178 ml	59.5	178
1/2 cup	118.5 ml	39.5	118.5
1/3 cup	79 ml	26.5	79
1/4 cup	59 ml	20	59
1 TBS	15 ml	5	15
1 1/2 tsp	7.5 ml	2.5	7.5
1 tsp	5 ml	2	5

1/3 cup heavy cream powder + 1 cup water = 1 cup heavy cream

Butter, Powdered

Measurements		Product (ml)	Water (ml)
US	Metric		
1 cup	237 ml	237	213
3/4 cup	178 ml	178	160
1/2 cup	118.5 ml	118.5	106
1/3 cup	79 ml	79	71
1/4 cup	59 ml	59	53
1 TBS	15 ml	15	13.5
1 1/2 tsp	7.5 ml	7.5	7
1 tsp	5 ml	5	4.5

1/4 cup + 3 TBS water to 1/2 cup butter powder = 1/2 cup = 1 stick

Margarine, Powdered

Measurements		Product (ml)	Water (ml)
US	Metric		
1 cup	237 ml	237	213
3/4 cup	178 ml	178	160
1/2 cup	118.5 ml	118.5	106
1/3 cup	79 ml	79	71
1/4 cup	59 ml	59	53
1 TBS	15 ml	15	13.5
1 1/2 tsp	7.5 ml	7.5	7
1 tsp	5 ml	5	4.5

1/4 cup + 3 TBS water to 1/2 cup margarine powder = 1/2 cup = 1 stick

Cream Cheese, Powdered

Measurements		Product (ml)	Water (ml)
US	Metric		
1 cup	237 ml	415	119
3/4 cup	178 ml	311.5	89
1/2 cup	118.5 ml	207	59
1/3 cup	79 ml	138	39.5
1/4 cup	59 ml	103	29.5
1 TBS	15 ml	26	7.5
1 1/2 tsp	7.5 ml	13	4
1 tsp	5 ml	9	2.5

To make 3 oz. of cream cheese use 10 TBS of cream cheese powder to 3 TBS of water.
To make 8 oz. of cream cheese use 1 3/4 cup cream cheese powder to 1/2 cup of water.

Fruit Powders

Banana, Powdered

Measurements		Product (ml)	Water (ml)
US	Metric		
1 cup	237 ml	55	237
3/4 cup	178 ml	41	178
1/2 cup	118.5 ml	27	118.5
1/3 cup	79 ml	18	79
1/4 cup	59 ml	14	59
1 TBS	15 ml	3	15
1 1/2 tsp	7.5 ml	2	7.5
1 tsp	5 ml	1	5

2 tsp banana powder + 3 TBS water = 3 TBS banana juice

Blackberry Juice, Powdered

Measurements		Product (ml)	Water (ml)
US	Metric		
1 cup	237 ml	55	237
3/4 cup	178 ml	41	178
1/2 cup	118.5 ml	27	118.5
1/3 cup	79 ml	18	79
1/4 cup	59 ml	14	59
1 TBS	15 ml	3	15
1 1/2 tsp	7.5 ml	2	7.5
1 tsp	5 ml	1	5

2 tsp blackberry powder + 3 TBS water = 3 TBS blackberry juice

Blueberry Juice, Powdered

Measurements		Product (ml)	Water (ml)
US	Metric		
1 cup	237 ml	55	237
3/4 cup	178 ml	41	178
1/2 cup	118.5 ml	27	118.5
1/3 cup	79 ml	18	79
1/4 cup	59 ml	14	59
1 TBS	15 ml	3	15
1 1/2 tsp	7.5 ml	2	7.5
1 tsp	5 ml	1	5

2 tsp blueberry powder + 3 TBS water = 3 TBS blueberry juice

Cherry Juice, Powdered

Measurements		Product (ml)	Water (ml)
US	Metric		
1 cup	237 ml	55	237
3/4 cup	178 ml	41	178
1/2 cup	118.5 ml	27	118.5
1/3 cup	79 ml	18	79
1/4 cup	59 ml	14	59
1 TBS	15 ml	3	15
1 1/2 tsp	7.5 ml	2	7.5
1 tsp	5 ml	1	5

2 tsp cherry powder + 3 TBS water = 3 TBS cherry juice

Lemon Juice, Powdered

Measurements		Product (ml)	Water (ml)
US	Metric		
1 cup	237 ml	55	237
3/4 cup	178 ml	41	178
1/2 cup	118.5 ml	27	118.5
1/3 cup	79 ml	18	79
1/4 cup	59 ml	14	59
1 TBS	15 ml	3	15
1 1/2 tsp	7.5 ml	2	7.5
1 tsp	5 ml	1	5

2 tsp lemon powder + 3 TBS water = 3 TBS lemon juice

Lime Juice, Powdered

Measurements		Product (ml)	Water (ml)
US	Metric		
1 cup	237 ml	55	237
3/4 cup	178 ml	41	178
1/2 cup	118.5 ml	27	118.5
1/3 cup	79 ml	18	79
1/4 cup	59 ml	14	59
1 TBS	15 ml	3	15
1 1/2 tsp	7.5 ml	2	7.5
1 tsp	5 ml	1	5

2 tsp lime powder + 3 TBS water = 3 TBS lime juice

Orange Juice, Powdered

Measurements		Product (ml)	Water (ml)
US	Metric		
1 cup	237 ml	55	237
3/4 cup	178 ml	41	178
1/2 cup	118.5 ml	27	118.5
1/3 cup	79 ml	18	79
1/4 cup	59 ml	14	59
1 TBS	15 ml	3	15
1 1/2 tsp	7.5 ml	2	7.5
1 tsp	5 ml	1	5

2 tsp orange powder + 3 TBS water = 3 TBS orange juice

Pineapple Juice, Powdered

Measurements		Product (ml)	Water (ml)
US	Metric		
1 cup	237 ml	55	237
3/4 cup	178 ml	41	178
1/2 cup	118.5 ml	27	118.5
1/3 cup	79 ml	18	79
1/4 cup	59 ml	14	59
1 TBS	15 ml	3	15
1 1/2 tsp	7.5 ml	2	7.5
1 tsp	5 ml	1	5

2 tsp pineapple powder + 3 TBS water = 3 TBS pineapple juice

Freeze-Dried Raspberry Juice, Powdered

Measurements		Product (ml)	Water (ml)
US	Metric		
1 cup	237 ml	55	237
3/4 cup	178 ml	41	178
1/2 cup	118.5 ml	27	118.5
1/3 cup	79 ml	18	79
1/4 cup	59 ml	14	59
1 TBS	15 ml	3	15
1 1/2 tsp	7.5 ml	2	7.5
1 tsp	5 ml	1	5

2 tsp raspberry powder + 3 TBS water = 3 TBS raspberry juice

Freeze-Dried Strawberry Juice, Powdered

Measurements		Product (ml)	Water (ml)
US	Metric		
1 cup	237 ml	55	237
3/4 cup	178 ml	41	178
1/2 cup	118.5 ml	27	118.5
1/3 cup	79 ml	18	79
1/4 cup	59 ml	14	59
1 TBS	15 ml	3	15
1 1/2 tsp	7.5 ml	2	7.5
1 tsp	5 ml	1	5

2 tsp strawberry powder + 3 TBS water = 3 TBS strawberry juice

Powders

Honey, Powdered

Measurements		Product (ml)	Water (ml)
US	Metric		
1 cup	237 ml	711	237
3/4 cup	178 ml	534	178
1/2 cup	118.5 ml	355.5	118.5
1/3 cup	79 ml	237	79
1/4 cup	59 ml	177	59
1 TBS	15 ml	45	15
1 1/2 tsp	7.5 ml	22.5	7.5
1 tsp	5 ml	15	5

3/4 cup honey powder + 1/4 cup water = 1/4 cup honey

Peanut Butter, Powdered

Measurements		Product (ml)	Water (ml)
US	Metric		
1 cup	237 ml	474	158
3/4 cup	178 ml	356	119
1/2 cup	118.5 ml	237	79
1/3 cup	79 ml	158	53
1/4 cup	59 ml	118	39
1 TBS	15 ml	30	10
1 1/2 tsp	7.5 ml	15	5
1 tsp	5 ml	10	3.5

2 TBS peanut butter powder + 2 tsp water = 1 TBS (add sugar and oil to taste)

Shortening, Powdered

Measurements		Product (ml)	Water (ml)
US	Metric		
1 cup	237 ml	237	237
3/4 cup	178 ml	178	178
1/2 cup	118.5 ml	118.5	118.5
1/3 cup	79 ml	79	79
1/4 cup	59 ml	59	59
1 TBS	15 ml	15	15
1 1/2 tsp	7.5 ml	7.5	7.5
1 tsp	5 ml	5	5

1 cup shortening powder + 1 cup water = 1 cup shortening (add oil for texture)

Soy Sauce, Powdered

Measurements		Product (ml)	Water (ml)
US	Metric		
1 cup	237 ml	158	237
3/4 cup	178 ml	119	178
1/2 cup	118.5 ml	79	118.5
1/3 cup	79 ml	53	79
1/4 cup	59 ml	39.5	59
1 TBS	15 ml	10	15
1 1/2 tsp	7.5 ml	5	7.5
1 tsp	5 ml	3.5	5

1 tsp soy sauce powder + 1 1/2 tsp water = 1 1/2 tsp soy sauce

Teriyaki Sauce, Powdered

Measurements		Product (ml)	Water (ml)
US	Metric		
1 cup	237 ml	158	237
3/4 cup	178 ml	119	178
1/2 cup	118.5 ml	79	118.5
1/3 cup	79 ml	53	79
1/4 cup	59 ml	39.5	59
1 TBS	15 ml	10	15
1 1/2 tsp	7.5 ml	5	7.5
1 tsp	5 ml	3.5	5

1 tsp teriyaki sauce powder + 1 1/2 tsp water = 1 1/2 tsp teriyaki sauce

Vinegar, Powdered

Measurements		Product (ml)	Water (ml)
US	Metric		
1 cup	237 ml	158	237
3/4 cup	178 ml	119	178
1/2 cup	118.5 ml	79	118.5
1/3 cup	79 ml	53	79
1/4 cup	59 ml	39.5	59
1 TBS	15 ml	10	15
1 1/2 tsp	7.5 ml	5	7.5
1 tsp	5 ml	3.5	5

1 tsp vinegar powder + 1 1/2 tsp water = 1 1/2 tsp vinegar

Worcestershire Sauce, Powdered

Measurements		Product (ml)	Water (ml)
US	Metric		
1 cup	237 ml	158	237
3/4 cup	178 ml	119	178
1/2 cup	118.5 ml	79	118.5
1/3 cup	79 ml	53	79
1/4 cup	59 ml	39.5	59
1 TBS	15 ml	10	15
1 1/2 tsp	7.5 ml	5	7.5
1 tsp	5 ml	3.5	5

1 tsp Worcestershire powder + 1 1/2 tsp water = 1 1/2 tsp Worcestershire sauce

Maple Syrup, Powdered

Measurements		Product (ml)	Water (ml)
US	Metric		
1 cup	237 ml	474	237
3/4 cup	178 ml	356	178
1/2 cup	118.5 ml	237	118.5
1/3 cup	79 ml	158	79
1/4 cup	59 ml	118	59
1 TBS	15 ml	30	15
1 1/2 tsp	7.5 ml	15	7.5
1 tsp	5 ml	10	5

2 TBS maple syrup powder + 1 TBS water = 1 TBS maple syrup

Wine Powder

Burgundy Wine, Powdered

Measurements		Product (ml)	Water (ml)
US	Metric		
1 cup	237 ml	237	237
3/4 cup	178 ml	178	178
1/2 cup	118.5 ml	118.5	118.5
1/3 cup	79 ml	79	79
1/4 cup	59 ml	59	59
1 TBS	15 ml	15	15
1 1/2 tsp	7.5 ml	7.5	7.5
1 tsp	5 ml	5	5

1 cup burgundy wine powder + 1 cup water = 1 cup wine

Chablis, Powdered

Measurements		Product (ml)	Water (ml)
US	Metric		
1 cup	237 ml	237	237
3/4 cup	178 ml	178	178
1/2 cup	118.5 ml	118.5	118.5
1/3 cup	79 ml	79	79
1/4 cup	59 ml	59	59
1 TBS	15 ml	15	15
1 1/2 tsp	7.5 ml	7.5	7.5
1 tsp	5 ml	5	5

1 cup Chablis wine powder + 1 cup water = 1 cup wine

Sherry, Powdered

Measurements		Product (ml)	Water (ml)
US	Metric		
1 cup	237 ml	237	237
3/4 cup	178 ml	178	178
1/2 cup	118.5 ml	118.5	118.5
1/3 cup	79 ml	79	79
1/4 cup	59 ml	59	59
1 TBS	15 ml	15	15
1 1/2 tsp	7.5 ml	7.5	7.5
1 tsp	5 ml	5	5

1 cup sherry wine powder + 1 cup water = 1 cup wine

PANTRY STUFFERS®
Rehydration Calculations
Made Easy
U.S. MEASUREMENTS
Tables provide dehydrated, freeze-dried & powdered
product substitutions for your favorite recipes
Wanda Bailey Clark

Flip your book over to find
U.S. measurements